You Can Write Children's Books WORKBOOK

TRACEY E. DILS

WRITER'S DIGEST BOOKS

CINCINNATI, OHIO

www.writersdigest.com

Visit our Web site at www.writersdigest.com for information on more resources for writers.

To receive a free weekly e-mail newsletter delivering tips and updates about writing and about Writer's Digest products, register directly at our Web site at http://newsletters.fwpubli cations.com.

08 07 06 05 04   5 4 3 2 1

Library of Congress Cataloging-in-Publication Data

Dils, Tracey E.
  You can write children's books workbook / by Tracey E. Dils.
    p. cm.
  Includes bibliographical references and index.
    ISBN 1-58297-248-6 (pbk. : alk. paper)
    1. Children's literature—Authorship. 2. Children's literature—Marketing. I. Title.

PN147.5.D57 2003
—dc21   2003065777
                                                                                          CIP

Edited by Michelle Ruberg
Designed by Sandy Kent
Production coordinated by Robin Richie

Author Biography

Tracey E. Dils has over twenty years of experience in publishing—as an editor, a publisher, an author, and a teacher. She is the author of over 35 books for children in a variety of genre, including biographies, nonfiction books, picture books, and how-to books. Her book, *You Can Write Children's Books*, continues to be a classic best-selling how-to book for those wanting to write for children. For her career achievements, she was awarded the Ohioana Award in Children's Literature in 1995. In addition to writing, Tracey enjoys inspiring writers, both adults and children, at schools and conferences. Tracey lives in Columbus, Ohio, with her husband Richard, and her children, Emily and Phillip.

TABLE OF CONTENTS

PREFACE

Three passions inspired me to write this book—my love for children's literature, my deep conviction that publishing is a business, and my need to inspire writers to the most noble writing cause there is: writing for children.

I hope that fans of my first book, *You Can Write Children's Books*, find this a *practical* companion. That book was theoretical; my goal in writing this book was to create a functional tool—a series of practical descriptions, sound advice, and creative and effective exercises that writers can use to practice and hone their skills. My grandest goal was to provide a course on writing for children in a book.

There are a number of themes running through this book that inform both the instruction and exercises in each chapter:

To me, it is essential that those of us who write for children are deliberate about the choices we make. Deciding why we write—specifically for children—keeps us grounded to our goals.

I don't believe writing is easy, and writing for children is no exception. In fact, it is my contention that writing for children is *more* difficult than writing for adults. You'll also discover that writing fiction for children has the same elements as writing fiction for adults. Knowing how fiction works through the effective interplay of character, plot, and setting is essential to writing for children. This book offers a thorough explanation of these elements and uses an example of a children's story to demonstrate their effective use.

Another theme you will discover between the pages of this book is the fact that children's publishing is a business—and it's becoming more business-like all the time. Submitting your manuscript, then, becomes less scary if you think of it like a business proposition. You are asking a publisher to take a risk—a financial risk—on your manuscript. Whether or not that publisher takes that risk has something to do with the quality of the story, but it probably has more to do with the economic conditions of the children's marketplace. You should find comfort in that fact, especially if a publisher rejects your work. It is likely the story just didn't make good business sense to them.

I've stressed the new direction of state and federal education initiatives in this book as well. These initiatives offer great opportunities for writers. Understanding the details of the initiatives isn't as important as understanding that children acquire knowledge through the written word. You, as a writer, are giving them that knowledge.

Finally, I hope you will sense great compassion between the lines of each chapter. Compassion is a strong emotion I feel for both the children who are my audience and the writers who are part of the larger writing community. I care deeply about issues that concern children, and I hope my work—both my writing and the work I do with kids—causes some small change in the way children perceive themselves.

For you, as a writer, I hope you will find some perspectives on your goals, on the craft of writing, and on the business of publishing. I hope you'll find support in your endeavor and that the advice I offer is sound and helpful.

And, if you find it so, I urge you to pass it on. The only way wonderful children's literature will continue to be created is by supporting each other as writers and by supporting the readers who are our audience. Please join me in that noble and worthy task.

How to Use This Book

Each of the eight chapters of this book offers explanations and discussions of the basic issues that face children's writers. In addition to the explanations, your will find:

The Writing Workout

These exercises have been provided so that writers will have a hands-on way to apply what they've learned. Many of the exercises in the workout offer a few suggested answers to get writers started. Some have been answered in their entirety as "example" worksheets.

Writing Group Grabber

Each chapter also offers a suggestion for a writing group exercise based on the chapter's topic.

Boxed Features

Boxed features offer additional information about the topic. These features work as quick reference tools for writers and as review for the topics presented.

1 THE WRITING ROAD MAP

If you are like most writers who want to write for children, you are passionate about what you do. You constantly think about writing for children and craft stories in your head. You talk to friends, neighbors, teachers—anyone who will listen—about your aspirations. You read voraciously yourself and to children, and are certain you can write a better book than the one you've just read aloud to your children. But have you ever stopped to think about why you want to write? And, specifically, why you want to write for children? You can enrich your writing if you do.

Think about the awesome power of children's books. When you write for children, you have the opportunity to change their lives. You can show them new worlds and give them renewed confidence by offering them characters that reflect their own experiences. You can give them a love of literature and story. And you instill in them one of the most important lifelong habits of all—reading.

How do you wrap your arms around this important mission? You must identify why you want to write for children and the steps you are willing to take to get there. Writing for children takes more than a strong desire. It takes an understanding of the impact your writing can have, along with an acknowledgment of your writing goals. It requires that you take your writing seriously rather than thinking of it as "just something you want to do."

THE POWER OF CHILDREN'S BOOKS

Good children's books:
- Help children enjoy reading
- Validate children's identity
- Offer an appreciation of language
- Promote emotional intelligence: discovering self-awareness, managing emotions, handling anxiety appropriately, motivating oneself, and developing sensitivity towards others
- Support oral storytelling
- Encourage an appreciation of art and story (especially in picture books)
- Inspire further inquiry
- Give readers a sense of power
- Reinforce learning and reading skills

One way to focus your thinking about writing for children is to create a kind of writing road map that states your mission as well as your goals. The mission part of the road map will help you take the time to identify why you want to write. Goal setting can help you organize priorities and stay on track. Together, these will constantly remind you of how important writing for children is to you.

Where do you begin? One way is to organize your road map around some basic statements about your desire to write, your understanding of the children's book industry, and how you value children in general. Consider the following statements, and think about how they can be integrated into your writing road map, as well as your personal and professional goals.

I will aspire to more than just being published. If you were to be completely honest with yourself about your writing goals, you would probably admit that one of those goals involves having your work published. Seeing one's work—and one's name—in print is a thrilling experience. And it is an experience no one can take away. If you write a book, it will likely outlive you. Your children, your grandchildren, and even your great-grandchildren may be able to find your books on the shelves of the library in years to come.

When you write for children, though, you need to aspire to a loftier goal than just being published. You need to acknowledge that your writing has unique power. You have the ability, through the stories you create, to directly impact the lives of your readers in a way writers for adults rarely do. As a children's writer, you have an awesome responsibility that extends beyond seeing your work in print or your name on the cover of a book.

I will work hard at my craft. One major misconception about writing for children is that it is somehow easier than writing for adults. This misconception is held not only by those outside the world of publishing, but by insiders as well. Perhaps those holding this false theory think writing for children is easier than writing for adults because the books tend to be shorter. Perhaps, as I've heard from even the most sophisticated critics, they think writing for children isn't "real" writing. The fact that actors and actresses with only passing knowledge of the craft can, based on their fame alone, churn out successful best-sellers for children does not help to dispel this notion.

But the fact is, writing for children is just as rigorous and requires the same—or more—attention to craft than writing for adults. Good writing requires that writers pay attention to the details, and to write, rewrite, and rewrite again to find a way to turn the English language into quality literature.

It is also true—whether one writes for adults or for children—that writing is not a talent one is born with. While some of us have a natural affinity for words and story, writing is not like perfect pitch. It is not something you have or don't have. Like anything worth doing, writing is work—lovely, creative, exciting, and important work. Acknowledging this fact is an important step in creating your writing road map.

I will respect my audience. If you want to write for children, you need to respect children—their sensitivities, their developmental needs, and their level of sophistication. Children know when adults—and adult writers—are talking down to them or being less than truthful. Young readers also realize when they are being hit on the head by a moral, or when a writer is underestimating their savvy. They recognize when writers oversimplify language or soften a story line inappropriately. It is important that you view children as intelligent, sophisticated, and sensitive. Challenge them in your use of language, plot, and character. And understand how your understanding of children and their development can affect your mission and your writing.

How do you develop a respect for your audience? One way is to make an effort to understand their development—how they reason, how they perceive themselves in the world, and what frightens and excites them—by reading the latest research on child development.

One of the most widely accepted theories of child development was developed by Jean Piaget. Piaget's theories have important implications for those who work with and write for children. Piaget postulated that children progress through several distinct stages of learning.

During the sensory-motor period from birth to around two years of age, children learn by experiencing the world through their senses and through movement. Recent research has shown that from birth, infants recognize patterns of sounds and that reading aloud to them can reinforce this sensory development. Visual discrimination—the ability to recognize and experience patterns in their environment and on pages of books—occurs in early infancy too, probably much earlier than even Piaget originally suggested.

In Piaget's second stage—the preoperational stage from ages two through seven—children begin to interact with the world through language, play, and drawing. Their thinking and reasoning is based on the experience of the moment, and they are the center of their own universe. They cannot easily comprehend the passage of time or cause and effect. Children in this stage respond to repetition and to the familiar in the books they experience. They generally do not respond to long, complicated plots and have difficulty developing empathy for a story's main character.

Piaget's third stage, which most elementary students experience, occurs from age seven and up and is referred to as the post-operational stage. In this stage, children understand the past and the present, as well as order and sequence. They enjoy more complex stories and identify with the characters in the books they read.

There are many child development theorists whose work can be helpful in understanding how children process information and experience literature. These include Bruno Bettelheim, Robert Coles, Maria Montessori, David Elkind, and Howard Gardner. A brief overview of their theories can be found in the special box on page 7.

There are other resources you can use to learn about child development. The National Association for the Education of Young Children is a national nonprofit

THE AUDIENCES FOR CHILDREN'S BOOKS

Children

Parents, Grandparents, and other adults who buy picture books for their children

Teachers who use books in the classroom

Librarians who make book selections at libraries

organization that offers resources and guidelines for the education of preschool children. Their guidelines include suggestions not only for what children should learn and when, but how to help them learn. Their publications, conferences, and other materials are well respected throughout the industry as the highest standard in terms of research and expert thought.

And, of course, spending time with children—analyzing what they say and how they feel—will help you recognize their developmental issues as well. Observing children informally at parks, malls, and playgrounds is one important way to reinforce your knowledge of child development. You can also seek out opportunities to formally work with children in church programs, and at libraries, schools, camps, and so on. These opportunities allow you to see the theories of child development in action.

Here's an example that impressed upon me the stages of child development and their implications for my writing. I was having a conversation with a four-year-old girl about what her father did for a living. "He goes to an office," she replied. When I asked what he did at the office, she thought and said, "He hangs the pictures that I drew him on his walls." She paused and added, "And sometimes he calls me and asks me how my day is going."

What did this conversation reveal? That four-year-old children, who are in the midst of the preoperational stage, see themselves as the center of their world. I knew this from my own study of development, but the conversation really made it hit home. I now use what I learned from that experience when I write for children six and below.

If you are going to write for children, it is essential that you develop a childlike perspective of the world. You may already feel you have this perspective. Many aspiring children's writers claim they want to write for children because they still feel like children themselves. But understanding what that means for your writing takes keen observation and a knowledge of the basics of child development.

I will work to become a part of the rich tradition of children's literature. Children's literature has a long tradition of excellence. By writing a children's book, you are joining this rich tradition. To understand the power of this genre and your role in it, you need to read the best and the greatest writers—and you need to analyze what made them so great.

To guide your reading, start with the award winners. The two most prestigious awards in children's literature are the Newbery and the Caldecott Medals. Established in 1922, the Newbery Medal is named for British publisher John Newbery and is the oldest award for children's books. (John Newbery has the distinction of being the first to publish books specifically for children). The Newbery is given every year by the American Library Association to the author who makes the most distinguished contribution to children's literature. Most Newbery award-winners are given to non-illustrated novels for middle grade or young adult readers.

Named for nineteenth-century English illustrator Randolph J. Caldecott, the Caldecott medal was first established in 1938. The American Library Association

Theories in Child Development

Bruno Bettelheim | The role of story, particularly of fairy tales and fantasy, in children's lives was the focus of Bettelheim's work. In his groundbreaking book *The Uses of Enchantment* Bettelheim claimed that fairy tales provided a kind of "magic mirror" of children's inner worlds. The reflection of a child's inner life in fairy tales, he claimed, enhanced a child's growth into maturity.

Robert Coles | Coles's research centers on the moral and political lives of children. His research indicates that while children base their moral development on concrete notions, children do, even in extraordinarily negative circumstances, develop moral sensibility and judgment.

David Elkind | Elkind's theories suggest that society is forcing children to grow up too quickly. In his book *The Hurried Child*, he postulated that children are being forced to develop a sophistication level that does not match their emotional development. Problem literature, literature that focuses on the ills of society, is detrimental to children because it forces them to deal with the problems of the world before they have dealt with the issues of childhood.

Howard Gardner | Gardner developed the theory of multiple intelligences. According to his work, there is no single intelligence, but rather eight separate intellectual abilities. These include linguistic, musical, spatial, logical, mathematical, kinesthetic, empathetic, and knowledge of self. His theories may help explain why some children are stronger in some areas of learning than others.

Maria Montessori | Montesorri contended that children learn naturally in environments that offer the proper materials. These materials include learning games, toys, household utensils, plants, and animals. Montessori also stressed the importance of exercise and motor abilities as complements to the learning process.

Jean Piaget | Jean Piaget developed the theory that children progress through various stages in their understanding of the world. A more thorough discussion of Piaget can be found on page five.

gives the award every year to the most distinguished picture book published in the United States. While the story is taken into consideration, the Caldecott medal is primarily given for illustrations. In addition to the medal-winners, the American Library Association also names Honor books for each award. Though Honor books do not receive the highest award, they are considered exceptional examples of children's literature.

THE MAJOR AWARDS IN CHILDREN'S LITERATURE

John Newbery Medal Awarded by the American Library Association to the author of the most distinguished contribution to American literature for children.

Randolph J. Caldecott Medal Awarded by the American Library Association to the most distinguished American picture book.

Hans Christian Andersen Medal Awarded every two years by the International Board on Books for Young People to a living author in recognition of his or her entire body of work. Katherine Paterson, Scott O'Dell, and Virginia Hamilton are among the Americans who have been awarded this honor.

Laura Ingalls Wilder Award Awarded by the Association for Library Service to Children to an author or illustrator who has made the most substantial and lasting contribution to children's literature. Beverly Cleary and Jean Fritz are among the winners of this award.

Coretta Scott King Award Given by the American Library Association to an African-American author or illustrator who creates a work of literature that promotes cultural values and acceptance.

Margaret A. Edwards Award School Library Journal and the Young Adult Library Services Association give this award to a young adult author for a body of work that helps teens understand themselves and society.

National Book Award for Young People's Literature The National Book Foundation gives this award in children's literature to an American author for quality children's literature.

Boston Globe-Horn Book Award The Boston Globe and Horn Book give these awards in three categories: picture books, fiction, and nonfiction.

The Golden Kite Award The Society of Children's Book Writers and Illustrators awards the Golden Kite to a member of the society who has created a distinguished work. J. Patrick Lewis is among the winners of this award.

Orbus Pictus Award The National Council of Teachers of English gives this award to a quality work of nonfiction published in the United States.

The Michael L. Printz Award The Young Adult Library Services Association awards the Printz to the best work of fiction, nonfiction, or poetry for readers between the ages of twelve and eighteen.

There are numerous other important awards as well. The Michael L. Printz award, named for a Kansas librarian who championed young adult literature, is given for the best work of fiction, nonfiction, or poetry for readers between the ages of twelve and eighteen. The Boston Globe-Horn Book awards are given yearly to works that achieve excellence in children's literature in the categories of fiction/poetry, nonfiction, and picture books. The Coretta Scott King award is given to the best book written by an author of African-American descent.

The American Library Association also identifies notable children's books. A list of notable children's books, by year, can be found on their Web site. The

International Reading Association, along with Children's Book Council, also identifies books of merit for young readers.

Another way to learn about the tradition of children's books is to take a course at a local college about children's literature. You'll not only learn about the great books of children's literature, but you'll also gain an understanding of how books are used in the classroom to reinforce learning and validate identity.

Reading award-winning children's books and classics is essential to understanding how children's literature is evaluated and judged by experts and by society at large. Most of the editors you approach with your manuscript will know the rich history of children's literature and aspire to publish books that meet the same standards. They know that award-winners and classics stay on the shelves of bookstores and libraries for decades, while the average title has a shelf life of three to five years.

I will learn the conventions of the genre and the audience. If you want to publish your work, you probably already know that the marketplace for children's books is highly competitive. Editors receive literally thousands of manuscripts a year from writers just like you, and most of those manuscripts are rejected. Many of these manuscripts are rejected because the writer has sent material that was simply inappropriate: The publisher may not publish that type of book, the book may not have been appropriate for the age group, or the work may not have fit an appropriate, accepted category. Knowing what the categories are—and what book formats fit into each category—is an important step in achieving publishing success.

You may feel that following these rules will stifle your creativity and that many of the books on the market today break these rules. The fact is, though, as a pre-published writer of children's books, you have more of a chance placing your book with a publisher if you follow the rules. Once you've published a book or two, you can probably break more of them.

For Children Ages 0-8

Before children learn to read or are able to read longer books, they experience books through what is probably the best-loved form in children's literature—the picture book. Picture books not only provide a rich literary experience, but they also help children make the connection between the printed word and the meaning; they introduce children to the essence of reading.

Picture books can be fiction, nonfiction, or poetry. They come in a variety of shapes, can include a novelty, like a pop-up or a lift-a-flap, and, as the name suggests, feature illustrations that are integral to telling the story. Though there is great variety within the picture book arena, all are of a standard length—usually 32 pages, less commonly 16, 24, or 40 pages. These lengths are not based on any aesthetic principles, rather they are multiples of eight, the standard amount of pages that printing machines can handle.

Since picture books are usually purchased by adults for children, they generally have to be appealing, at some level, to adults as well as children. Sentimental stories and stories that rely on nostalgia have this dual appeal. Stories with educational themes appeal to adults and, if they are entertaining enough, to children as well. While picture books are most commonly found on the bookshelves in the homes of families with young children, they are also used extensively in the classroom—beginning with preschool and often extending into the intermediate grades.

For Children Ages 6-10

Children who are learning to read are ready to experience several different kinds of books.

Early readers are designed for children who are just beginning to read. They feature limited, age-appropriate vocabulary, and photographs or illustrations that help the young reader recognize, or decode the words in the story. They often feature repetition of phrases, so that the reader can master the phrases and predict what will happen next.

Many early readers are "leveled" and allow children to progress through various difficulty levels. Early readers written for classroom use usually conform to educational standards regarding word recognition. They are generally leveled through an educationally-sound leveling system, such as the program named for U.S. developers Fountas and Pinnell. Early readers sold through retail channels are leveled in a more general way and rely on plot line, repetition, and illustration cues to help the child read the story. Early readers, usually 32-48 pages (around 500-1,200 words), are not usually organized into chapters. They usually contain four-color illustrations.

Chapter books are the earliest forms of novels. They are designed for children who are reading beyond the early reader stage but not yet ready for full-length novels. They are usually three to five chapters in length and may contain simple illustrations. While each chapter in the book features the same set of characters, the chapters are usually stories in themselves with their own beginnings, middles, and ends. Like early readers, conflict in chapter books is generally understated and the story relies on settings, routines, and characters that are familiar to the reader.

Middle grade novels are for readers in the third, fourth, or fifth grade—who are ready for novel-length books. These are the years children become voracious readers. The unprecedented success of the Harry Potter series is due, in part, to the fact that the novel was aimed at this "golden age" of readers.

Middle grade novels deal with the issues children this age are experiencing: coming of age, school situations, and friendship issues. They are conflict-driven and generally focus on a single main character. They range from the very realistic to fantasy. Historical fiction—fiction set in another era that includes true events of that era—is popular for middle grade readers as well.

The subject matter in middle grade novels ranges from very light to very serious. The conflict, as well, can be relatively frivolous or very grave. Whichever direction a middle grade novel takes, it's important for you as the writer of that novel, to treat the conflict as if it is *very* important to the main character. You need only remember your own middle grade years to understand this notion. Conflicts that seem unimportant to you now—problems with friends, wanting something you couldn't have, feeling awkward because you weren't good at something—were desperately important to you then. When you write about such conflicts, treat them with the same emotional intensity you felt when you were that age.

At this age, children also enjoy nonfiction. Early readers and chapter books can be either fiction or nonfiction. There is a large market for nonfiction reference books based on topics popular among children or taught in schools. These topics can range from dinosaurs to the mummies of ancient Egypt. Books about careers, animals, and different cultures are also popular.

For Children Ages 10 and Up

Young adult novels are read by older children, ages ten and up. These novels focus on more adult themes and content, and may feature identity issues, romance, and fantasy. Young adult novels are conflict-driven and deal realistically with the issues that young adults are facing. Like the conflicts in young teens' lives, the conflicts in young adult novels can be hard-hitting and dramatic.

There are generally two age categories for young adult novels. Younger young adults, readers ten to twelve years old, generally look for serious stories in novel form, but the content of the novels and the overall style is fairly straightforward. An older category of books for young adult readers, ages thirteen and up, is more sophisticated and stylized than those for younger grades. Many of these books cross over into the adult market.

An unusual phenomenon in the category of older young adult fiction is a genre called the graphic novel. These novels are completely illustrated throughout, often with a Japanese "anime" style. While some in the literary community dismiss graphic novels as just a sophisticated comic book, it is a literary category that is capturing the interest and attention of both reluctant and avid young adult readers.

Young adult novels are generally merchandised in their own sections, outside of the traditional children's book department. This is no surprise. Young adults consider themselves more sophisticated than children and have outgrown the children's sections of most bookstores and libraries.

I will determine the tools I need and assemble them. An important step in developing your road map is to determine the tools that you will need to write effectively and efficiently. To do this, you need to take into account your lifestyle and your creative rhythm. If you have a busy lifestyle—driving children in carpools or traveling extensively—you may decide to invest in a laptop computer. Some of my best work has been done "on the fly," on my laptop. I wrote *Cat Characters— A to Z* in the lobby of an ice rink while my daughter took skating lessons. It was only because I had a laptop and a dictionary that I could take advantage of what was a short, but precious, period of time for my writing.

You also need to pay attention to the cycle of your creative energy. You may be a "night writer," with creative urges coming in the evening and extending through the night. Or your creativity may be sharper in the early morning hours. While it's

Child Development 101

Infancy Through Toddler

Developmental characteristics:

- Short attention span
- Focus on self
- Use of senses to explore environment
- Formation of early language skills
- Need for trust in human relationships
- Development of basic self-help skills

Infants and toddlers need books that:

- Feature rhymes, lullabies, songs—anything with repetitive language
- Focus on the senses through touch and feel elements
- Have visual elements illustrated in vibrant, recognizable pictures
- Can be enjoyed in small spurts
- Show toddlers succeeding at daily routines without adult intervention

Preschool Through Kindergarten

Developmental characteristics:

- Develops language rapidly
- Active, but short attention span
- Focus is still on self, but develops curiosity
- Builds knowledge through experience
- Seeks stories that are reassuring
- Begins to understand what is right and wrong

Books for preschoolers and kindergartners should:

- Feature rhyme, cumulative patterns, nonsense tales, or stories without words that can be "told" by the child
- Be able to be read in a single sitting and involve child's participation
- Be told through a single viewpoint
- Help child enjoy educational concepts: colors, shapes, counting
- Encourage imaginative play

Primary, ages 6-7

Developmental characteristics:

- Increase in attention span
- More curious about outside world
- Beginning to understand the passage of time
- Beginning to separate fantasy from reality

- Learning empathy
- Developing sense of humor
- Striving to accomplish skills—takes pride in development

Books for early school age children should:
- Offer rich language
- Feature longer stories that are episodic
- Support an understanding of the passage of time
- Use fantasy and make-believe
- Feature characters kids can identify with
- Offer surprise endings, turn-around tales, and comedy

Middle Grades, ages 8-11

Developmental characteristics:
- Concerned with peer group acceptance
- Develops personal moral standards
- Shows empathy
- Looks for role models outside of family and school
- Develops interest in specific activities such as sports or music
- Begins to challenge authority

Books for middle grade children should:
- Provide opportunities for reading as an enjoyable leisure activity
- Offer stories that deal with peer group acceptance
- Feature a sense of justice
- Allow readers to identify intimately with characters
- Focus on specific subject matters
- Promote independence

Young Adult, ages 10 and up

Developmental characteristics:
- Self-concept and identity continues to grow
- Peer group becomes more important than family
- Sensitive to relationships and human emotions
- Think self is the center of attention and problems are unique
- Interest in sexuality

Books for young adults should:
- Focus on identity
- Feature peer group situations
- Allow reader to experience emotions vicariously
- Focus on a single character and that character's development
- Acknowledge sexual and romantic attraction

HOW TO FIND A WRITERS GROUP

Contact your local SCBWI Group

Consult the arts section of your local paper

Check bulletin boards at libraries, community centers, and bookstores

Inquire at bookstores

Contact literary centers

Inquire at colleges and universities in your area

helpful to acknowledge your own cycle, be cautious about using it as a crutch. There will be times when you have to deviate from your optimal writing schedule just to get the writing completed.

Tools are more than dictionaries, thesauruses, and laptop computers. They also have to do with human resources. As you embark upon your mission, keep in mind that there are others who are anxious to help you along the way. Other writers, of course, can serve as sounding boards and critics, helping you to revise and hone your work. Less obvious but just as helpful sources of support and advice include children's librarians, booksellers, and teachers.

Many writers find that a writers group is an essential tool as well. Writers groups generally meet on a regular basis to critique each other's works. For many writers, a regular meeting is like a due date. They know they must have a piece of writing ready for a meeting, and this motivates them to get it done.

Writers groups can provide more than writing discipline, though. When writers get together, they can share market information, offer each other support and encouragement, and celebrate successes.

And, of course, there are children themselves. Many writers feel that an effective way to assess their work is to get direct reaction and criticism from their readers. They bring their work into classrooms and read it out loud. The children are almost always delighted. After all, when they are being asked by the author herself how they feel, they are less apt to be critical.

A better way to assess your work with children is to be "incognito." Ask a teacher or another individual to read your work out loud without acknowledging the fact that you are the author. Watch the reaction of the children. Don't be as concerned about whether or not they like the work. Instead, observe if they laugh at the right places, seem absorbed in the story, and follow the plotline. Ask the teacher to have the children to retell the story afterwards. Did they understand the story?

I will learn the rules of submitting manuscripts. Just as there are certain rules for the categories of children's stories, there are also some rules that guide the process of submitting your work to a publisher. You'll increase your chances of being published if you adhere to these rules. Once you know what the rules are, they are not difficult to follow. Most publishers publish their own guidelines for submissions. These guidelines will likely indicate what kinds of manuscripts the publisher is looking for and how the publisher prefers to have them submitted. You can find a publisher's guidelines on their Web site, or you can request them through the mail.

In general, most publishers prefer to see picture-book manuscripts and early-reader manuscripts in their entirety, accompanied by a cover letter. Their preference is that the manuscript itself be sent, without illustrations, even if you are a professional illustrator. For chapter books, middle grade novels, and young adult novels, their preferences vary—they may want to see a proposal in the form of an outline, a sample chapter (generally the first three chapters), and a cover letter. (More detail on the submission process can be found in chapter eight.)

I will take chances. As with most important tasks, writing for children involves taking chances. In fact, the very act of submitting your work for publication takes phenomenal courage. In many ways, as a writer, you are your work. If your work is rejected, it may feel as if you are being rejected.

But if you don't take the chance to submit your work, you simply won't be published. Publishers aren't in the business of knocking on your door and asking you for your manuscript. If you are to get your work into the hands of children, you have to take that chance.

Another way you will be required to take a risk as a writer is in the genre you choose to pursue. Most children's writers want to write picture books, but you may enhance your craft and broaden your publishing opportunities if you consider trying other categories. There is always a need for good writers of nonfiction, for example. Stories, poems, word games, jokes, and other kinds of writing are published in many of the popular children's magazines. Taking a chance by trying something outside of your comfort zone can be a powerful turning point on your writing road map.

I will treat my writing seriously. Many aspiring writers are enthusiastic about their writing, publishing opportunities, and ideas for best-selling books, but they fail to commit to making their dreams a reality. Some use the excuse of "not enough time" or "not enough uninterrupted time" to write. Others claim their manuscripts haven't been thoroughly critiqued by their writing group. Writers struggle over their knowledge of the marketplace, with cover letters, with the rules of submission, or with not having an agent (though agents are not always required in the children's market), all of which holds them back. These writers may be fine writers, but they are not making their writing a professional priority.

Professional writers make time for their writing, and they find ways to more effectively use the time they have available to them. Professional writers may take advice from their writing groups, but they rely on their own judgment when revising and polishing their manuscripts. And professional writers know the business of the marketplace and keep up-to-date with that business.

There are a number of ways that you can keep up with what is going on in the children's book industry. Industry publications such as *Publisher's Weekly* and *School Library Journal*, publish articles about what is happening in children's publishing, as well as book reviews of the latest published books. *The Horn Book Magazine* is a journal dedicated to children's books and features reviews as well. The *Children's Writers' & Illustrator's Market*, published every year by Writer's Digest Books, offers a comprehensive list of publishers and their needs. The Society of Children's Book Writers and Illustrators (www.scbwi.org) is a professional organization for children's writers and illustrators that offers a newsletter and other publications, as well as regional and international conferences about writing and publishing.

What's the next step? Now that we've worked through some initial ideas about what it takes to write for children, it's time to consider how you will put these ideas into action. Let's take them one at a time and consider how you can use them to create your own mission and goals to inspire your writing.

YOUR WRITING ROAD MAP

1. **I will aspire to more than just being published.** What are some of the important reasons you want to write for children, reasons that have nothing to do with being published? Make a list and then organize it in order of your personal priority. You can use the list that has been started here, or you may want to write your answers on note cards, so you can shuffle your priorities and reorganize them.

   I have a message to send to my readers.

   I want my writing to inspire a lifelong love of reading.

   I want to impart values—spiritual, moral, or other.

   I have a personal story to tell.

2. **I will work hard at my craft.** What exactly does working hard at the craft of writing mean? You probably are already using some techniques and practices that feel like work to you, but you may not recognize that there are other ways to hone your craft. Consider the possibilities below and add your own to the list.

   I will hone my grammar and other mechanical skills.

   I will take advantage of a class, seminar, or other opportunity to focus on writing technique. (Consider online classes as an option.)

   I will revise a piece of writing that I feel is "finished" one more time.

3. **I will respect my audience.** As I've suggested, respecting your audience—the children for whom you are writing—is best accomplished by getting to know children and their developmental needs. List some ways that you plan to get to know you audience.

   I will volunteer in a setting that involves children.

   I will observe a single child in a group setting.

I will find and study a source of child development and identify how it will affect my writing.

4. **I will work to become a part of the rich tradition of children's literature.** It's essential you recognize that children's literature is more than a pastime. It's an institution. List the ways you will develop your knowledge of children's literature and your place in its tradition

I will read five Caldecott winners from five different eras.

I will analyze five Newbery Award winners.

I will read three books about the tradition of children's literature.

5. **I will learn the conventions of the genre and audience.** Beyond what is offered on these pages, what else can you do to learn about a category of books and its special requirements? Add your own ideas to this list.

I will choose a single category of children's books and learn the "rules" of that category.

I will identify the ways in which a successful picture book follows or breaks the rules.

I will speak to one "expert"—librarian, teacher, writer, editor—about the category of books I am exploring.

6. **I will determine the tools I need and assemble them.** As I've suggested, assembling the "tools" often requires writers to do a kind of inventory—both of their creative style and of the resources they have available. Below, list some ways you will assess your needs and prepare your tools.

I will track my creative style and develop a writing schedule accordingly.

I will develop professional contacts I can rely on for industry information and advice.

I will develop an effective way to get a reaction to my work from children.

7. **I will learn the rules of submitting manuscripts.** Many manuscripts are rejected each year—not because the writing is bad—but because the writer failed to submit the work to the appropriate publisher in the appropriate way. Publishers' own guidelines often specify exactly what they are looking for and the way they prefer submissions to be prepared. List the steps you will take to learn more about what publishers require from submissions.

> I will use the Children's Writer's & Illustrator's Market to identify publishers who publish the kind of book I want to write.

> I will review guidelines from three publishers.

> I will read representative picture books from the publishers I have identified.

8. **I will take chances.** When you submit your manuscript, you are taking a chance. How will you handle that risk? How will you assess other opportunities for your writing? Consider these possibilities and add yours.

> I will submit one manuscript to a book publisher.

> I will try a new category of writing.

> I will research opportunities outside the realm of children's books for my work.

9. **I will treat my writing seriously.** Taking your writing seriously means you schedule time for writing and take advantage of the professional tools available to you. List the ways you intend to take yourself seriously as a writer.

> I will investigate joining a professional organization like SCBWI.

> I will commit to writing X hours or X pages a week.

> I will read one magazine or journal that addresses the publishing industry.

To finalize your writing road map, take a look at the lists you have created. Put a star by the items on the list you feel you can accomplish within the next six months. Then put it all together in a commitment statement you can use to guide your writing on a regular basis.

Here's a framework to get you started:

I want to write for children because I want to (list the top three reasons you've identified in question number one). _____

I will accomplish this goal by _____
(list all of the items that you realistically feel that you can address in the next six months).

Keep this writing road map close at hand—maybe next to your computer or tucked in your journal. When you get lost or overwhelmed—due to lack of writing time, lack of confidence in your own writing, or confusion over what your writing goals are, pull it out and reread it. It will continue to direct you to where you want to go.

WRITING GROUP GRABBER

Consider the various commitments we've discussed in this chapter. Each member of your writing group will no doubt have different responses to each commitment. Ask each member to rank the eight statements in order of priority. Then, suggest that each member develop goals under their top priority in writing. Have members share their goals, then exchange them with one member of your group. At each subsequent meeting, members will check in with their goal-setting partners about what they are doing to achieve the goal and what they can do to meet the goal more effectively.

2 THE WRITING HABIT

The writer's most difficult task is to develop a serious writing habit. This is as true of professional writers as it is for those who are just starting out. There is a built-in fear that comes with sitting down with a blank piece of paper or a computer screen. To fill that screen with words means that you are letting yourself become vulnerable. You aren't just talking about writing for children any more—you are doing it. And someday, deep inside, you know you will show your work to someone else, submit it to a publisher, and risk rejection.

ACKNOWLEDGE THAT WRITING IS WORK

When you read children's books out loud to a child, you no doubt appreciate the book for its sense of story, its use of language, or its overall message. Unlike adult novels that usually feature intricate plot twists, multiple characters, and messages that work on a variety of levels, children's books seem as if they would be simple to craft.

But writing a children's book is every bit as difficult—more so, most claim—than writing an adult book. The more quickly you acknowledge that good books are not supposed to come easily, the sooner you will be prepared to face the work of writing head-on.

I have not done a formal survey on this, but I suspect that most children's writers are parents. In fact, becoming a parent is what inspired me to write for children in the first place. That means that most children's writers have at least *one* other job.

The writers I know that are most successful at developing a writing habit recognize that writing is just as important as their other jobs. To treat writing as a second or third job requires a complicated juggling act, to be sure, but once you embrace the notion that writing is your second or third job, you will begin to make time for it in your busy life. After your daily routine, you may be tired, lack energy, and probably just want to call in sick, but you won't. It's your job, so you will show up.

Formal Programs

One good way to develop a writing habit is to enroll or participate in a formal writing or instructional program.

Correspondence schools, such as the Institute of Children's Literature, offer one way to develop a disciplined writing habit. Barnes & Noble University provides online courses on writing for children. Many colleges and universities have creative writing courses as well, although those courses tend to be general writing classes rather than specifically focusing on writing for children. (In fact, you may encounter a bit of snobbery at universities about the value of writing for children.) Community centers and literary centers may also offer formal study in writing for children. And there are several graduate level masters of fine arts programs that offer graduate work in creative writing for children.

Writers retreats offer a different take on the writing habit. Writers retreats focus on giving writers time to write by isolating them. They may also offer social events, critiquing, and professional speakers, but a significant portion of time is spent just writing. The most well-known retreat for children's writers is the Highlights Foundation Writers Workshop at Chautauqua (www.highlightsfoundation.org).

On retreat, a writer may break through writer's block, develop new ideas, and hone his writing technique. If you are a member of a writers group, you may want to suggest this experience as a project for your group. If you have the time—and can find a place to go outside your own environment—you may want to plan a personal writing retreat for yourself.

IT TAKES LONGER THAN YOU THINK

No matter what you are writing, no matter what draft you are on, writing takes longer than you think it will. What is so discouraging is that most people—editors, included—have no idea how long it really takes to produce a solid story. What's more frustrating is the fact that children's books, which are shorter than adult books, can take longer to write than adult books. Mark Twain's famous adage, "If I had more time, I would have written a shorter letter," applies to almost all of the writing you will do.

As you develop your writing habit, forget immediate gratification. The first words that you put down on paper may seem brilliant as you write them, but when you go back, it's likely that they will disappoint you. Don't let that stop you in your tracks.

Go back to your writing map and revisit all the reasons you want to write for children. Then get back to work as soon as you can.

GO GRADUAL

One way to develop an effective writing habit is to go about it just as you would go about developing any habit—start slowly and build gradually. Psychologists suggest that we go about developing physical exercise programs precisely this way.

Begin by planning regular writing sessions. Be realistic about how often you plan these sessions. Writers who try to write every day, especially at first, often become completely discouraged and give up. Consider your own schedule and determine how much time you can commit. Make sure, though, you are realistic about the amount of time you can commit to a regular writing schedule, even if it is only a "writing day" every week.

Begin with ten to fifteen minutes a session. Train yourself to sit at your writing place and write for the full amount of time. Use a timer to keep yourself honest. Don't worry about the quality of your writing at this point. It's the habit you should focus on developing.

You can consider what you put on paper (or your computer) at this point freewriting or you can choose to work on one of the exercises from this book. If you're stuck, try writing something personal—a letter to a friend, your own biography, your reaction to your favorite book.

Gradually add additional time until you build to a full hour. After you've mastered an hour, move on to an hour and fifteen minutes—until you are writing a full two hours at a time. Why two hours? Most of us can carve out two hours—even if it is in the early morning or in the late, late evening. If this seems impossible to you, consider the time you spend on leisure activities. How much television do you watch? How much time do you spend chatting with friends on the phone or surfing the Internet? Take that time back. Make it productive, writing time.

Two hours is also a magic number because it is approximately the time it takes to really get into a piece of writing. Eventually, you'll feel the rhythm. You'll settle down in around fifteen minutes, focus for a good hour or so, take a break, return, and then finish up. At the end of the session, you may feel as if you want to keep at it. If you do, you've mastered the writing habit. But don't keep writing until you become stale. Some of the writing you will do takes place in your head, after you've sat at your computer. If you keep thinking about your story after you've written it, you can be assured that you are well on your way to developing a writing habit that works.

NOW SET NEW GOALS

Once you are comfortable sitting for two hours—with occasional breaks, of course—set yourself different kinds of goals. These goals should be focused on what you produce, not how long you write. Set a goal for how many pages or how many words you will write within that period of time. Keep in mind that your goal doesn't necessarily have to revolve around creating a children's story. You can spend time sketching out a character for a middle grade story, planning a plot for young adult novel, or developing a setting for a picture book. Whatever you produce, try not to judge what you are producing. (Remember that you've put aside the need for instant gratification—at least where your writing is concerned.) Focus on the fact that even if what you are writing doesn't end up in your final story, you've produced something that you can revise at a later date.

SET NEW GOALS AGAIN

You are producing—and you are producing some material that is likely workable. The next step is to set goals for each individual writing session and to record those goals before the session starts. It's not unlike planning a menu or a schedule. Let's say your writing session is Tuesday. On that day, you intend to complete a rough draft of a picture book manuscript. Write that goal and keep to it.

You may find it helpful to purchase an appointment book to keep track of your writing appointments. When I first began writing full-time, I bought an appointment book that showed an entire week at a time, broken down by fifteen minute segments, from 8 A.M. to 9 P.M. I planned my writing time using this calendar. Eventually I was recording other activities that supported my writing—school visits, writers conferences, critique groups. The calendar became a valuable record for tracking my schedule and reporting work-related activities when it came to tax time.

WRITE ON THE FLY

Now that you have developed a solid writing habit, you will probably develop the ability to write on the fly. Writing on the fly means that you can use smaller amounts of time—even five minutes—to attend to writing. Consider revising a draft of your work as you are waiting to pick up your child from sports practice. Reread a draft as you are drinking your morning coffee. Do a quick character sketch after your lunch break. The writing you do may not be your best work, but it will form the basis for what will become your best work when you have larger spans of time.

"ATTITUDE" AND YOUR WRITING HABIT

One impediment to the writing process is the inability to acknowledge that writing is a valuable activity. With all the important things going on in your life, it may seem superfluous, even self-indulgent. This is especially true when you write for children, an activity many of your peers and even your family may see as a flight of fancy.

It is important, then, to develop "attitude," writer's attitude, as it were, so that the work you are doing seems valuable and purposeful.

You can start by developing attitude concerning how you talk about yourself as a writer. When others ask about your writing or what you are working on, what is your response? Do you actually downplay your writing, conveying your own less-than-positive attitude about what you do and its importance? Hopefully, you stand up straight, hold your head high, and say these four important words: "I am a writer."

Identifying yourself as a writer means calling yourself a writer. You may identify

23

yourself in several other ways as well—as a teacher and a father, for example. Add writer to that list and you will be surprised at how positively those around you will respond and how you will feel about yourself.

BEING ALONE

A very important step in developing a writing habit is being able to be alone and comfortable with your thoughts. Writing is a lonely business. Many writers are loners by nature, but many writers are surprisingly gregarious and need the support of friends, family, and loved ones. The key to balancing your natural gregarious personality with the loneliness of writing is to compartmentalize time. Try to commit to keeping your writing life—your solitary life—separate from your social life. Schedule your time so that you block out specific amounts of time for writing and specific times to interact with people. It sounds a bit cold and mechanical, but it will keep you from wasting your writing time talking on the telephone to a phone solicitor just because you are desperate for conversation.

IDENTIFY YOUR ENEMY

We all have our favorite enemies that keep us from writing. Yours may be the television set, the refrigerator, the cobwebs in the corner that you don't notice until you sit down at your computer, or the lawn that needs to be mowed. Indeed, I often have observed that my own house is never as clean as when I have a book deadline looming.

Identifying your writing enemies is an important step in fighting them. If you know that when you find yourself empty of ideas at your computer you want to turn on your television, unplug it or move it. If you are distracted by housework tasks, learn to shut them out. And don't forget one of the biggest time-sappers of them all—the Internet. Many writers surf the World Wide Web in the pretense of doing research. Beware of this time-waster. It's easy to get caught in writer's chat rooms, visiting publisher's Web sites, and researching various publishing opportunities. Before you know it, you have frittered away all of your valuable writing time.

VARY YOUR WRITING PLACE

While it's important to create a consistent writing space within your home or apartment, you may find that it is effective to vary your writing space from time to time. If you aren't being productive at home—either because of the distractions or because you're bored with your environment—try someplace new. Local libraries are terrific places to write. Most have desks or carrels with outlets so you can plug in your laptop if needed. Many have computers you can use as well. The biggest advantage of libraries, of course, is that they are full of books—for reference and for inspiration. You will also have the opportunity to watch kids interact with books and to chat with children's librarians about trends in children's books. Finally, you will be able to check out the many periodicals for children and the professional magazines for the publishing industry.

Coffee shops offer a different kind of writing experience as well, and most of them don't mind if you write at their tables—as long as you buy their coffee!

DEAL WITH THE VOICES

When you are alone with your computer or a piece of paper, you may hear voices of self-doubt in your head. They may tell you your writing isn't worth it or that it will never make the cut. It's important to shut out these voices and stay focused on your writing. One way to shut them out is to review your writing road map and to make sure that you are on the right path. Another way is to keep focused on your goal for each session.

The good news about voices: There are also good ones that overshadow the negative ones. Many writers—children's writers among them—find that as they get further into their writing, they begin to hear the voices of their characters. That usually means that they are really getting to know their characters. Other writers, myself included, simply "hear" a narrative voice that guides the tone of what they are producing. If you hear voices like these, don't think you are ready for the loony bin. Consider yourself lucky. You have gained true focus on your writing. And consider yourself particularly lucky if you have difficulty shutting out the voices after you've stopped writing. If you continue to hear those voices, you are actually doing the work of writing when you aren't sitting at your computer.

MAKE THE BEST USE OF YOUR WRITERS GROUP

Writers groups are a great way to meet other writers and to share resources and information. Many writers groups critique each other's work; these critiques provide a valuable way to get feedback on your work. Keep in mind, though, that some writers groups (as well as writers conferences) can get off track. While discussing your work and critiquing the work of others is important to the writing process, it is not really writing. Make sure that you balance the time you spend in your writers group with the time you spend writing.

Keep in mind that a critique from a writers group is only as good as the member of the group. If most of the members of your group haven't been published yet, you are being critiqued by your peers. Keep their criticism in perspective and remember—they have just as much experience as you do.

Writers groups can become more effective if they focus their critiquing. Be clear about what you are looking for from the group. Are you looking for affirmation, or are you looking for specific comments about the manuscript? State your critique goals up front, and the critique and your reaction to it will be more valuable.

Some writers groups have made the conscious decision to make critiquing only a part of what they spend their time doing. They also spend time researching and discussing the marketplace, participating in group or individual writing exercises, or volunteering in a public service capacity that is related to writing and literacy. Other writing groups relegate the critiquing part of their session to communicating on the Internet or by phone. This frees up meeting time for other activities.

YOUR WRITING PLAN

Developing a writing habit—like any habit—is easier if you have a plan. Use this worksheet to draft your writing plan. I've completed one worksheet for you to show you the kinds of things you might include.

Day one: Monday, April 1

Time: 10:00 P.M.

Goal: 15 minutes

Writing topic: A description of my daughter's first day of school from my viewpoint.

Evaluation: Accomplished full 15 minutes.

Feelings about experience: Difficulty actually sitting for that long. Kept feeling that I had something else to do. Worried about why the dog was barking outside.

Feelings about writing: Writing wasn't my best effort. It didn't feel productive or get me toward my overall goal.

Goal for day two: 18 minutes. Write on same topic through a child's point of view.

Day one:

Time:

Goal:

Writing topic:

Evaluation:

Feelings about experience:

Feelings about writing:

Goal for day two:

SETTING NEW GOALS

Once you are able to write for an hour or two at a time, it's time to set new goals. Now you are going to set a goal that reflects what you are going to produce in the period of time you are writing. The goal needs to be achievable; you need to be accountable to the goal.

Goal (word count):

What was accomplished:

Time:

How you feel:

WRITING ON THE FLY

Bring a draft with you the next time you expect to have some downtime, whether it's waiting for an appointment or to pick up your child from soccer practice. Try and shut out all outside noise and focus on your draft.

What did you accomplish? I read aloud the picture book manuscript in an attempt to revise it.

How do you feel about what you accomplished? I felt a little ridiculous reading it aloud. I did mark places where I thought the language was a bit rough.

When is the next time you might write on the fly? When I am waiting for the oil in my car to be changed on Tuesday.

IDENTIFY YOUR ENEMY

Write down the top five enemies to your writing habit and how you will combat them. Here is one example.

The refrigerator. I'll take my laptop and write at my local library.

 WRITING GROUP GRABBER

1. Volunteer for a literacy organization. You can volunteer to tutor a nonreader or work on a fund-raiser. (Consider a fund-raiser for First Book, a national organization that provides infants with a book of their own.)
2. Develop a mentor program for young writers. Consider working one-on-one with writers or inviting young writers to a session of your writing group.
3. Visit a literary landmark. Plan a trip to a literary site in your community.
4. Attend a lecture or an autograph session by a children's writer.

5. Form a mock Newbery or Caldecott committee and vote on your favorites. See how they stack up against the actual choices.

6. Make a monthly commitment to submit your work. Once a month, walk to the post office together and send something out—a query letter, a manuscript, or a request for guidelines. Then go celebrate!

3 YOUR WRITING PREFERENCES

If you've been thinking about writing for children, you probably have some idea concerning what you want to write about. You may have been inspired by a single story idea, a topic that you've been dying to explore, or an experience that your own child has had. You've probably identified the reasons that this story idea resonates with you and why it should resonate with children.

But where do you go from there? When most writers think about writing for children, they immediately think picture book, but, as we've seen, there are other formats to choose from. And within the broad categories we have identified, there are subcategories to consider as well.

One of the most important decisions you need to make at this stage is how to flesh out your idea to match it with the appropriate format. The story you want to tell may not be suitable for a picture book. Likewise, you may have your heart set on writing a middle grade novel, but the subject matter you have chosen may not be complex enough to sustain an entire novel.

Remember, too, that while you may have a story that you are determined to tell, there are many experiences, topics, and sparks of inspiration. Stay open to all kinds of ideas, but always keep in mind your own writing abilities, interests, and goals so that you can determine the direction you want to go.

GETTING TO KNOW THE CATEGORIES

To decide what type of book you'd like to write, you should become familiar with the basic conventions of that particular type.

Picture Books

A picture book is generally defined as a book in which all or part of the story is told through illustrations. As was stated previously, almost all picture books are 32 pages. Occasionally, picture books are slightly longer (40 pages) or slightly shorter (24 pages). Board books, which are picture books printed on sturdy, stiff board for younger children, are generally 16 pages.

Within the picture book category, there is great variation. Some picture books have no words at all. Children follow the story by looking at the pictures only, making up their own narrative and telling their own story. Other picture books contain full stories as long as 5,000 words. Most picture books fall somewhere in the middle at 500-1,000 words.

In general, there are three broad categories of picture books, although there are many variations and many good picture books cross categories.

Concept Books. Concept books teach a concept—anything from counting and the alphabet to overcoming a common childhood dilemma like a new baby or a fear of the dark. Their goal is to help a child understand her world or to extend and reinforce her knowledge of a particular subject. Concept books are developmentally appropriate. Books about counting, for instance, are aimed at children ages three to four who are developmentally ready to learn to count.

Story Books. Story books tell a story with a distinct beginning, middle, and end. They start with a conflict that kids will understand. This conflict is generally introduced in the story's opening paragraph. The story then follows the main character as he or she goes about solving that conflict. As in all good fiction, the main character in picture books generally solves the problem and undergoes some kind of character growth as the conflict is resolved.

Novelty Books. A novelty book relies on a sense of novelty to engage the reader. The novelty might be a pop-up, a lift-a-flap, or some unique treatment of the artwork or illustrations. The prevailing opinion among book reviewers and children's literature experts about novelty books is that the novelty should provide some sort of function in the book. In other words, the novelty should exist for something more than just the novelty's sake.

Subject Matter and Theme

Picture books offer variety in subject matter just as they do in format. While the subject matter should be appropriate for children, there are certainly picture books that challenge that notion. In general, though, picture books:

- Are about children. Often the main character is a child.
- Include references to a world children understand and feel familiar with.

- Create empathy for the main character by showing situations that readers can identify with.
- Are careful not to include any situation that would encourage the reader to do something reckless or dangerous. Picture book readers are young and impressionable. For example, a book about running away that does not suggest the consequences would be irresponsible.
- Are lyrical in their choice of language. Because picture books are usually read aloud, their tone and word choice are especially important.
- Are visual in their approach. The orchestration between the narrative and the visual episodes is what makes a picture book work. The best picture books vary their settings and feature action that can be visually represented.

Are You a Picture Book Writer?

If you want to write a picture book, you need to be a visual thinker. You need to be able to imagine what the illustrations for your book are going to look like and be able to organize your story in visual episodes, episodes that generally follow a chronological progression. At the same time, if your book is accepted by a publisher, you have to be willing to let your vision of the book go. The illustrations are the domain of the art director at the publishing company, and, however much you end up liking the final product, the illustrations are almost always different than you imagined them.

Picture book writers also need to have an ear for language. Whether the language chosen for the story is literary or playful in tone, the language chosen should always do more than just narrate the story. If you are fascinated by words and the rhythms of read-aloud stories, you are likely to be sensitive to language choice.

Because picture books need to work on at least two levels—one for children and one for adults—writers of picture books need to have a sense of the issues that concern their young audience and their adult counterparts. While picture books need to be child-centered in perspective, they need to offer elements, messages, or themes that will resonate with the adult reader and customer.

Early Readers

Early readers, sometimes called leveled readers, are generally 32, 48, or 64 pages long and are consistently at a $6'' \times 9''$ size in the bookstore market. (There are educational and institutional versions of first and leveled readers as well, and these vary in size.) Early readers are aimed at children when they are just developing reading skills. (Children this age are often called "emergent readers.") Emergent readers crave "real books" instead of the picture books that were read to them when they were younger. Early readers, then, tend to look a little bit more sophisticated than picture books, can be fiction and nonfiction, and are generally heavily illustrated. The illustrations provide clues to the meaning of the story for the reader. These books vary in length from around 500-1,500 words, depending upon the reading level.

Early readers depend less upon story than picture books or novels. They often rely on a repetitive pattern, like this:

> I like cake.
> My twin brother likes cookies.
> I like cats.
> My twin brother likes dogs.

The child will be able to master the story fairly easily because of the repetitive pattern. The book will likely end with some sort of simple twist:

> I like vanilla ice cream
> My twin brother likes chocolate ice cream.
> But we both love birthday parties!

(The twist, of course, is that their birthday is on the same day.)

Early readers might also focus on a cumulative pattern, much as the story *I Know an Old Lady Who Swallowed a Fly* or *The House that Jack Built*. Every time something new is added to the cumulative pattern, the reader repeats the new item, plus the item that was mentioned previously. In so doing, the child is beginning to master the words in the story.

Whichever technique an early reader uses (and there are others besides the ones mentioned, including a straight story line), the books always feature simple text and straightforward sentence structure. The plot is also simple and straightforward, but it moves along at a nice clip.

Can You Write Early Readers?

Those who choose to write early readers are generally more successful if they know how children go about acquiring the ability to read. If you have ever taught or helped in a classroom that includes children who are beginning to read or if you have observed your own child acquiring those skills, you are one step closer to knowing how best to write a good early reader.

You don't have to become a reading specialist to write early readers, however. You also don't need to get too caught up in reading methodology, phonics, etc. What is most important is that you read as many books as you can in this genre so that you can model your writing appropriately.

There are also several tools that can be helpful in constructing early readers. A number of good books list the words that children are supposed to recognize at various age levels. One of these lists, the Dolch Word List, is used to develop reading programs in schools but can be adapted for use in trade books. The *Children's Writer's Word Book* is a terrific resource for those writing first readers as well. It is both a word list and a thesaurus, so that writers can make alternative selections for more difficult words.

If you use word lists like these, don't be afraid to throw in a whopper of a word once in awhile, especially if it can be understood in context. Children who are beginning to read hate books that sound or feel babyish. Challenge them occasionally. Most emergent readers are up to the challenge.

Chapter Books

Chapter books provide the transition for children from early readers to middle grade books. They are either fiction or nonfiction, although the majority of chapter books are fiction. The chapters may build upon each other in terms of plot, but they are fairly self-contained. Each chapter offers an action-filled incident. Each chapter may also feature its own conflict and resolution.

Chapter books tend to be about contemporary situations in contemporary settings that are familiar to readers. They rarely feature historical or exotic (a foreign country) settings. Chapter books frequently use humor as a device to enliven the plot and retain the reader's interest. They may also offer the opportunity for their readers to recognize themselves—and to laugh and make light of their own situations or behavior.

Chapter books typically feature passages of dialogue. Dialogue is used to move the story along and to break up the denseness of the page. Dialogue is discussed in detail in chapter five.

Are Chapter Books for You?

Writing a chapter book may be the perfect category for you if you have a story in mind that is episodic in nature and that occurs in a familiar setting. It will require that you become very familiar with your setting as it appears today. Keep in mind that chapter books are contemporary. If you haven't visited your setting—whether it's a summer camp, school, swimming pool, or amusement park—it's a good idea to, so that your setting will feel genuine and real to your reader.

Your dialogue will need to sound contemporary and genuine as well, so it's just as important to listen to children talk to each other to pick up on the rhythm and patterns of their speech.

Middle Grade Novels

Middle grade novels are aimed at independent readers or fluent readers. They are generally 14,000-20,000 words and are organized into longer chapters than chapter books. Rather than being self-contained, each chapter builds on the one before it as traditional fiction plots do. Middle grade novels fall into a wide range of categories: traditional novels with contemporary settings, historical novels, light horror books, mysteries, and fantasies.

For many children, middle grade books are the first time readers make reading choices on the basis of gender. There are "boy" books and "girl" books. General wisdom says that girls will read books about boys or girls, but that boys will tend to select books about boys only. Whatever the case, middle grade readers are making more decisions based on advice from friends.

Middle grade readers are also into collecting. Series books are very popular because middle graders like to collect all the books in a particular series. Choosing a series book also offers a kind of guarantee. If readers like the first book in a series, they are likely to enjoy reading the rest of them.

Are You Ready for Middle Grade Readers?

To write for middle grade readers, you really need to know your audience, especially if you are writing a novel that has a contemporary setting. You need to know where they hang out, how and what they talk about, what they worry about, what they are wearing, and so on. Middle grade kids are savvy consumers and can immediately spot products that are less than genuine.

If you want to write for middle grade readers, you also should have a knack for dialogue, fast plot pacing, and realistic characters. Again, it's a good idea to spend time reading the offerings in this genre to get a sense of whether the category works for you.

Young Adult Novels

Young adult novels are generally longer than middle grade readers, from 25,000 words to as long as 50,000 words. In bookstores, they are often called "teen novels." Young adult novels take more experimental forms than any other category. They range from traditional, contemporary stories, like *The Outsiders* by S.E. Hinton, to rather bizarre and unusual fantasies, like the bleak novel *The Giver* by Lois Lowry. And, as mentioned earlier, graphic novels are extremely popular in the young adult category.

Publishers are paying renewed attention to young adult novels, in part because of the buying power of teen consumers. Research also indicates that, contrary to what many people think, some 60 percent of teens read for pleasure. Publishers are taking advantage of these trends by pushing young adult novels with special book promotions, Web sites, and other programs to make sure that they reach this audience effectively.

Can You Write for Teens?

If you are attracted to offbeat writing, then pursuing young adult novels may be for you. Teens understand the notion of how a traditional plot works but they are open and hungry for books that offer alternatives to what they have studied in English class.

More than any other category, though, writing for young adults requires that you really know your audience and that you have a keen sense of where young adults see themselves developmentally. The process of moving from young adulthood to adulthood is a painful one, and at some level, all young adult novels deal with that passage.

In addition, the emotional lives of young adults are generally in a frenetic and exaggerated state. Young adults are feeling emotions they have never felt before, and they overanalyze these feelings, usually feeling them more deeply than they did as children or will as adults. In his insightful book about teens and reading, *Exploding the Myths: The Truth About Teenagers and Reading*, author Marc Aronson concludes that during the early and middle adolescent years, young adults desire and feel desired for the first time in their lives. It's a powerful and complex combination, one writers need to explore and acknowledge.

Matching Subject Matter and Theme

One of the best ways to understand your own writing preferences is to discover what you are most passionate about, to determine what excites and engages you. Begin by asking yourself these questions:

- What do I spend my time thinking about?
- What do I like to read about?
- What topics are close to my heart?

After you've defined your options, take time to ensure that your choice of subject matter is appropriately matched to age group and format. Consider these possibilities and how they connect to the appropriate age level.

Tell Your Story

Mining your personal history for inspiration for your children's book is a great way to get your imagination flowing. It works well as inspiration for all of children's book categories, especially for middle grade novels and young adult books. However, it is a bit of a double-edged sword. On the positive side, you know your personal history intimately. You can no doubt recall the details of the important events of your childhood and the sensory details surrounding the events. You probably can remember the intense emotions you have had at various points in your life. When you base your writing on personal history, you are, quite simply, writing what you know the most about.

On the negative side: The events of your childhood are just that—events. They are not a story with a logical beginning, middle, and end. More importantly, depending upon the event or emotion, you may not have experienced the level of character growth that is necessary to sustain a book.

I often tell writers that the heart of writing is knowing the truth—and then lying about it. If you use personal experience as the basis of your story, you need to be willing to go beyond the facts of the experience and make it resonate with real meaning. You will need to distance yourself from the experience, and view it as an outsider so you can appropriately turn it into a story.

It is just as necessary to exercise caution when basing a story on something that happened in your own child's life. Again, an incident is simply not a story with a beginning, middle, and end. Just as important, your child is not like all children.

In order to make your child's story work as a picture book, you need to make it universal so readers can see themselves in the story.

If you choose to write about an incident that happened to you or your child, keep this in mind: Literature is tidier than life. It improves upon life experience. The story you write should lend meaning and understanding to your personal history, by enhancing that history. And, in so doing, it will almost always have to stray from the actual facts of the incident. The magic in using personal history as a basis for your story involves turning truth into fiction.

Special Needs and Situations

If you are involved with a child with a special need or a special situation, you may feel compelled to write about that need. Writing about special needs works particularly well in picture books if treated at a level that picture readers can understand. It also can become a compelling theme in young adult novels, since teens are often experiencing life-changing events and feeling the emotions associated with those events in a deep and complex way.

You may want to write about special needs for all the right reasons—to promote a better understanding of that special need, to give the issue some much-needed attention, or to validate the child who is suffering from this need. The needs can range from anything from autism and Down's syndrome to dealing with divorce or the aging of a grandparent.

The first thing to consider if you want to write about a special needs issue is this: how universal is it? The readership for a book about autism—even as widespread as autism is—is probably only people who are in contact with someone with the condition. The book might be used in schools to help children understand a child who may be different, or it might be used in support groups or therapeutic settings. Keep in mind that the readership and the number of publishers who will give the book a serious look will be limited. To increase your chances of publication, make the story line as universal as possible so it can speak to as many people as possible.

If you are writing a book about a subject that children experience more commonly—divorce, for instance—your story is likely to have broader appeal both to readers and to publishers. Again, you want to make the story as universal as possible, focusing on broad themes instead of making it specific to your situation.

Be careful not to pile one problem on top of another. When you write about a specific need, focus on that need and that need only. If your main character just lost a grandparent, focus on the loss rather than adding additional problems. Imagine how chaotic a story would become if the child who lost a grandparent was blind, had a parent who was handicapped, and lived in a homeless shelter. This may seem far-fetched, but I've actually seen stories like this, usually from writers who know of a situation where this has actually happened. (This is an example of fiction failing to transcend actual facts.)

Teach Your Children Well

Today, more than ever, children's book publishers are emphasizing an educational mission as well as literary integrity. Federal legislation and parental interest in children's achievement is fueling this trend. Informational books, books that enhance standard curricular areas, and picture books that engage children in the reading process are among the types of books enjoying a spike in sales from schools, libraries, and individuals.

Books that rely on educational concepts are generally aimed at preschool and lower grades and, as such, are particularly appropriate for picture books and chapter books. Children of middle grade and young adult age are seeking to read for pleasure not for edification, although reference books about topics they are learning about in school, as well as books that deal with careers, fashion, and sports, are popular at older grade levels.

If you know the field of education—either because you are a teacher or because you are keenly aware of what your own children are learning in school—you have a built-in way to garner information about these trends and to integrate that information in your writing.

If you don't know the field of education intimately, there are easy ways to become informed. Start with what you know about how children learn. Before going to school, they need to know certain skills: the alphabet, numbers and counting, the concept of opposites, and colors and shapes. Take some time out to observe preschool and kindergarten classes, and you will quickly pick up on the concept that children need to be "school-ready" simply by observing what and how the teacher presents the lessons in the classroom.

Your state's department of education has a Web site that will enhance your knowledge of educational standards. Most state Web sites tell you what "units" are taught at what grade levels. Almost all first and second graders, for example, are offered a teaching unit on the ocean. Knowing this may spark fiction and nonfiction book ideas in you. (Another excellent resource for learning about age-specific knowledge is E.D. Hirsch Core Knowledge series. This series of books, starting with, *What Your First Grader Needs to Know* and progressing through grade six, provides a succinct description of the fundamentals of good education by grade level.)

On department of education Web sites, you'll also learn what holidays are celebrated throughout the school year. President's Day, Valentine's Day, and Black History Month are important school holidays, and books that tie into these holidays are widely sought after.

The Web site will also offer information on proficiency testing—what grade the tests are administered in, what the tests mean, and what subject matter is tested. Because proficiency testing is so significant to student success, tying your manuscript into subjects that are widely tested will give you an advantage when you submit it. This doesn't mean that you have to write about the test itself. If you discover, however, that all fourth graders need to know certain social studies concepts, you may use those concepts as inspiration for your writing.

The Great Outdoors

If your passion is the outdoors, you have found a natural inspiration for your writing. Books that encourage a love and respect for nature are not only relevant, they enjoy popularity in the marketplace. These books may be fiction or nonfiction, and focus on animals, human beings and their relationship to the environment, or natural settings. The great outdoors is a great inspiration for every book category, from picture books through young adult books. Books for younger readers tend to use nature as a backdrop for stories, where books for teens, including the adventure novels by Gary Paulsen, focus on survival and classic human vs. nature struggles.

EXPLORE THE POSSIBILITIES

Good Books About Nature and Science

I Took a Walk, Henry Cole

Pond Year, Katherine Lasky

In the Tall, Tall Grass, Denise Fleming

Henry Hikes to Fitchburg, D.B. Johnson

Owl Moon, Jane Yolen

Great Books That Were (Probably) Based on Personal History

When I Was Young in the Mountains, Cynthia Rylant

Roxaboxen, Alice McLerran

A Band of Angels: A Story Inspired by the Jubilee Singers, Deborah Hopkinson

A Chair for My Mother, Vera B. Williams

To Kill a Mockingbird, Harper Lee

Books That Incorporate Humor

Click, Clack, Moo: Cows That Type, Doreen Cronin

Miss Nelson is Missing!, Harry Allard

The Stupids Die, Henry Allard

The True Story of the Three Little Pigs, Jon Sciezka

Amelia Bedelia, Peggy Parish

The Great Quillow, James Thurber

In the Rain with Baby Duck, Amy Hest

Martha Speaks, Susanne Meddaugh

Multicultural Stories

How My Parents Learned to Eat, Ina Friedman

Black is brown is tan, Arnold Adoff

Roll of Thunder, Hear My Cry, Mildred D. Taylor

The Talking Eggs, Rovert D. San Souci

The Watson's Go to Birmingham—1963, Christopher Paul Curtis

The Birchbark House, Louise Erdrich

Grandfather's Journey, Allen Say

Pablo's Tree, Pat Mora

Growing Up

Many strong and rich children's books, in particular picture books and young adult novels, focus on the transitions children experience as they grow up and the relationships that are important to them along the way. If these two issues resonate with you—and you can deal with them in a creative and sensitive way—you may find yourself drawn to this kind of book. Picture books that integrate either one of these two themes generally offer soft, sentimental stories, but the sentimentality is rarely overdone. Typically, these books center on family and sibling relationships, family history, or cultural issues.

Inspirational

If you are spiritually oriented, you may want to discover how to turn your spirituality into an engaging story for children. There are inspirational books in every book category. The themes of inspirational books can be directly based on scripture, but usually they are not. Instead, they are often quiet stories that depend on a kind of spiritual sentimentality. The stories sometimes deal with life's transitions, such as death and birth. The story's true message, often called the "takeaway," appears at its conclusion.

The Melting Pot

As our world becomes more and more diverse, there will be a greater and greater need for stories that celebrate and provide information about other cultures. Multicultural themes are appropriate for every book category. Today's multicultural books take many forms: contemporary stories, folktales, and stories based on historical events.

Folktales are a great way to expose children to other cultures through subtle means. The basic story framework is generally familiar to young readers, but the multicultural details are not. Folktales also contain universal themes. The story of Cinderella, for instance, has served as the basis for many wonderful picture books based in various cultural settings. The story has also been told for middle grade readers in the wonderful novel, *Ella Enchanted*, by Gail Carson Levine.

Multicultural issues need to be treated with sensitivity. Stories that deal in ethnic stereotypes—the kid from an Asian country who is smart, the African-American child who is good at basketball, the Native American youngster who has a special bond with nature—will be seen as stale and shallow. Stories with messages about races getting along or different cultures coming to understand each other through stereotyped themes are, as a general rule, not effective because they do not sound genuine. (This would include books in which a family of a different race moves to a community, isn't initially accepted, and somehow makes others accept them through some heroic feat.)

Write What You Read

Another way to choose your subject is to think about your own reading preferences. What kinds of books do you like to read (even if they are for adult audiences)? Are you drawn to mysteries, romances, historical fiction? All of these genres have a presence in children's literature. Mysteries are a popular genre for middle grade readers. Romance is a theme in young adult novels. Historical fiction is found in book categories for both middle grade and young adults. If you read many books of a certain kind, it's likely that you know how they work—and you'll probably have better success with a genre you love.

What Children Want

Of course, there are myriad other topics and themes that are the inspiration for children's books. And, while it is important to tap into your own passions and interests, it is at least equally important to tap into what kids are passionate about. If you can find the intersection of your passion, children's interests, and established book categories, then you will most likely find yourself creating your best—and most relevant—work.

Track Commercial Trends

To determine what trends are currently popular in the world of kids, pay attention to what's popular in other mediums. Check the movie schedule for the most popular kid's movies. Know the television shows they are watching as well as the music they are listening to. Analyze the trends in other retail areas: discount stores, department stores, and the like. And, of course, review the current best-selling books for children.

Another good way to keep abreast of the trends is to watch what is going on with older children. Eventually, all trends filter down from adults or older children to younger ones. The book business provides many examples of this phenomenon in both fiction and nonfiction genres. The inspirational Chicken Soup for the Soul books started as adult books, were made available for teens, then midteens, and now, are available in picture book form. The same is true of the best-selling business book *Who Moved My Cheese?* by Spencer Johnson and Kenneth Blanchard; an adult, teen, and kid's version were all published.

What Children Do

Children like reading about kids who do the same things they do. Incorporating and writing about children's favorite activities is one way you can engage them in your story. Keep in mind, too, that children can most easily understand what they know firsthand. A young reader, for example, will likely understand or have experienced riding a bike, playing baseball or soccer, going to school, and having a babysitter. It's not likely they have experienced driving a race car, flying an airplane, or visiting a foreign country, which means those topics might not make the most engaging story ideas.

While this generally holds true for young readers, it is not necessarily true for middle grade or teen readers. In fact, older readers often seek books that allow them to experience vicariously what they cannot experience in real life.

Children Want to Grow Up

While children like to read about what is familiar to them, they also enjoy reading about characters who are slightly older or have slightly more freedom than they do. This allows them to experience being older as they identify with the characters. When developing your characters for middle grade and teen readers, then, it's a good idea to create characters who are slightly older (and never younger) than your intended audience. A fourth grader, for instance, will read about another fourth grader—but will really enjoy reading about a fifth or sixth grader. On the other hand, they will certainly be reluctant to read a novel that centers around a third grader.

Leave Them With Laughter

Children love humor in literature, especially in picture books, chapter books, and middle grade novels. There are two kinds of humor that are irresistible. The first is the turn-around-tale. In a turn-around tale, things are exactly the opposite of what they should be. A monster is frightened, a pirate is very unpiratey, or a witch cooks up wonderful meals instead of creating deadly spells. In a similar vein, children also enjoy reading about adults who aren't all that bright. (Amelia Bedelia is exactly this kind of character.)

Children also love wacky words: made-up words, words that just sound plain funny, or phrases that are used in a different way. They also enjoy surprises and simple uses of irony. They also recognize and giggle at exaggerations. This is natural—kids exaggerate all the time. They enjoy seeing that familiar trait in the books they read.

Know How Children Live

Today's children are growing up under conditions that are probably far different from your childhood. A large number of children live in single-family homes, and many are being raised by grandparents. Also, more female parents are working than ever before. In many families, it's the father who stays home and fulfills the obligations of the child's daily needs. Knowing how children really live can inform your story, give it a sense of the familiar, and impress a potential editor.

THE TOUGH TOPICS

Within all of these creative ideas, it's only fair to acknowledge the kinds of books that are most likely going to be tough sells to editors. They are:

- Anthropomorphized animals
- Personified objects
- Books written in rhyme

Anthropomorphized animals are talking animals that behave as human beings do. You're probably thinking that you remember lots of stories from your childhood in which animals talked. You're right, of course, but most editors find them objectionable.

Their objections may arise from the fact that books featuring talking animals feel dated, but it is more likely because these books are difficult and complex to write, and editors rarely see manuscripts that are written well. Writers who use talking animals as characters need to ensure that the world they are creating is consistent. If animals are behaving entirely as human beings, they need to be placed in a human environment and interact with other animals who are behaving as human beings. Children can make the leap that animals can behave as humans, but they become confused when those humanlike creatures can interact with real human beings. It's all more complicated than it looks; editors know this and tend to regard most talking animal manuscripts with a the same negative feel.

Personified objects are inanimate objects that become real, such as *The Little Engine That Could*. Again, there is a rich and long tradition of this kind of book in children's literature, but editors are distrustful of books that use personified objects and may reject them without reading the first page. As in the case of anthropomorphized animals, these books are hard to write well. As a writer, you are asking your young reader to actually *believe* that an inanimate object has feelings. It's a tough sell to editors and to readers, even readers with the most vivid imaginations.

Rhyming stories are objectionable, not because editors don't like rhyme, but because most rhyming stories they receive are not well-written. (This may seem unfair, but considering the huge numbers of manuscripts editors receive every day, they have to draw the line somewhere.) If you do want to write a rhyming story, you need to rely on rhythm as much as rhyme. You also need to use natural language and not complicate sentences just for the sake of rhyme. The best tools for writing rhyme are a rhyming dictionary and a thesaurus. If the rhyme you've selected doesn't work in your story, then you can turn to the thesaurus for another word that means the same thing and try and rhyme it. As a prepublished author, though, no matter how good your rhyming story is, you may have trouble getting an editor to give it a serious look.

ANALYZE THIS

In order to understand how to structure a book, it is a good idea to rely on what other writers have done. By analyzing their techniques, you will become better at analyzing your own writing and determining where your work fits in.

Picture Books

Choose at least three to six picture books and determine what their dominant characteristics are and in which categories they fit. Once you have determined that, analyze the books, looking for these features:

Concept Books

1. What concept is the book trying to teach? Is the concept:

    Related to behavior (sharing, jealousy, anger, etc.)

    Related to education (alphabet, numbers and counting, time, etc.)

    Related to a special need (dealing with a disease or an emotional situation such as divorce, etc.)

    A combination of the above

Story Books

1. Who is the main character? Is the main character:

    An adult

    A child

    An animal character

    Other

2. Does the main character grow and change? Identify the major way the character has changed:

    Overcomes an emotion

    Learns to rely on self/develops self-confidence

    Comes to a new understanding of situation

    Other

Novelty Book

1. What is the novelty?

    Pop-up

Lift-a-flap

Sound from a computer chip

Find hidden object (as in *Where's Waldo?*)

Other

2. How does the novelty function in the book?

Exists for the novelty's sake only

Teaches a concept

Furthers the story

First Readers

1. Does the book use repetitive language?

2. What are the phrases that are repeated?

3. How do those phrases change from page to page?

4. Does the book use cumulative language?

5. What is the pattern of the cumulative language?

6. Does the book appear to use vocabulary that is geared to a young reader's understanding? Identify where it seems to stray from that vocabulary and challenge the reader.

7. Does the book offer a twist at the end? What is that twist?

Chapter Books

1. Does the book have a conflict? Is the conflict about:

School

Friends

Other

2. Is the book based in a familiar setting?

3. Identify the episode in each chapter of the book.

Middle Grade Novels

1. Which category does the book fit into:

Contemporary novel

Mystery

Historical fiction

Horror

Other

2. Who is the audience?

Boys

Girls

Both

Ages

3. How old does the main character appear to be? Is the main character older than the intended reader?

4. Analyze a single chapter. How much of the chapter is dialogue?

How much of the chapter is narrative?

Identify the ways the book uses humor.

Young Adult Novels

1. Does the major conflict center around:

Identity

Romance

Life-threatening or life-changing situation

Other

2. Can you define the conflict as the main character overcoming:

A character flaw

The opposition of another character
Opposition from society

3. Does the novel use traditional narrative or does it use an experimental form?

FIND YOUR PASSION

As a brainstorming exercise, list some subjects, themes, or hobbies you feel strongly about. Be as specific as you can. I've made some suggestions to get you started.

The treatment of animals

How kids are treated at school

Basketball

Now list some themes, subjects, or hobbies that you think children are crazy about. Here are some examples:

Pets

Friends

Dinosaurs

Now try and match up the items on the first list to the second. On the list that I have made, I can find several interesting story ideas. You may find it best to list these ideas in "what if" form so that you can take them in several different directions:

What if dinosaurs played basketball?

What if a new kid at school had no friends?

What if a pet was being mistreated?

Finally, see if you can combine the "what if" statements with the three categories of picture books. Here are examples:

A concept book (maybe it involves counting) about dinosaurs that play basketball

A story book about a pet that is mistreated

A novelty book about a new kid at school with no friends (maybe it's a lift-a-flap and under each flap is a new friend)

BACK TO SCHOOL

List the basic skills that young children need to know in school. Here are examples:

Counting

Following directions

Recognizing the alphabet

Colors

Shapes

Opposites

Combine these with some of the interests you've listed for yourself and for children, and see how many story ideas you generate.

TELL YOUR STORY

The best books that are based on personal history do not reveal the true nature of that history. Instead, they weave a story about a personal event, much of which is fiction. Recall some events that were pivotal in your young life. I've begun the list to get you started:

First day of school

The death of a pet

The birth of a sibling

After you've completed the list, identify several incidents you have always wanted to write about. Jot down some notes about how those incidents might have been different had they been experienced:

1. In contemporary times

2. By someone older or younger than you

3. By someone in a different culture

It's Only Natural

Books that rely on science and nature themes deal with their subject matter at a child's level. Often, the plot itself may revolve around a theme about our natural surroundings, but the story ultimately suggests something to the child about his or her own world. Make a list of natural events a child experiences. Here are some examples:

Thunderstorm

Caterpillar turning into a butterfly

The passing of the seasons

Blizzard

Going fishing

After you've completed the list, consider what emotions children have about these experiences. Then, consider how you can use this list to make your story resonate with children. Here are examples:

Thunderstorm: fear

Caterpillar turning into a butterfly: loss

The passing of the seasons: _____

Blizzard: _____

Going fishing: _____

It's All About Change

Make a list of the transitions that children go through from ages four through eight.

Starting school

Getting a pet

Giving up a favorite object (a blanket, for instance)

Now make a list of the important relationships that children have in this same time period.

Grandma

Mother

Sibling

Connect each transition to a relationship to create plot ideas. I've suggested the first one below.

> How would a grandmother help a child starting school?

SPIRITUAL AND INSPIRATIONAL

For children, spiritual and inspirational issues are often connected to institutions, such as a church or synagogue, or to religious holidays. Make a list of experiences that a child might have in a religious institution or during a religious festival or holiday.

> Celebrating a spiritual holiday with a relative home from the army
>
> Serving a meal at church for the homeless
>
> Participating in a church Christmas pageant

What spiritual or inspirational themes might be connected with these events?

> Celebrating a spiritual holiday with a relative home from the army—Thanksgiving
>
> Serving a meal at church for the homeless
>
> Participating in a church Christmas pageant

THE POT OF MULTICULTURAL GOLD

Stories that evoke multicultural themes take many forms. Consider your own cultural heritage.

1. Make a list of ways that your culture or your family's heritage are different than the mainstream. Consider food, celebration, sense of history, stories and legends, etc.

   > large family reunions
   >
   > stories about favorite relatives
   >
   > German potato salad

2. Now make a list of story ideas based on what you discovered about your own culture.

   > large family reunions—story about how an outsider (foster child) might feel

stories about favorite relatives—historical fiction about Aunt Mary's voyage to the U.S.

German potato salad—story about a grandmother handing down the tradition to a granddaughter

YOUR READING PREFERENCES

What was the last good book you read for children?

> *Emily* by Michael Bedard

What was the last good book you read for adults?

> *The Lovely Bones* by Alice Sebold

What was your favorite book as a child?

> *Charlotte's Web* by E.B. White

Ask a child what his or her favorite book is.

> *Harry Potter and the Sorcerer's Stone* by J.K. Rowling

List five things that all of these books have in common. Then think about ways these common themes can be used as inspiration for the kind of story you want to write.

- All involve themes of triumph over adversity.
- All are fiction.
- All are about a world I knew little about.
- All focus on death and the meaning of death.
- All focus on a single character.

WHAT CHILDREN KNOW

Write down five popular movies for children.

> *Holes*

Write down five popular television shows for children.

> *Lizzie McGuire*

Write down five trends that children are experiencing

> "Gypsy", 70s style clothes

Write down five popular books for children.

Captain Underpants by Dav Pikey

Now look for commonalities among them. What do these shared traits suggest for the theme of your next story? How might you work these themes into a story without allowing the story to become dated?

What are five things that children participate in?

Soccer

Ballet

How might you weave a story around one or more of these issues?

Character's championship soccer game conflicts with her ballet recital. How will she resolve it?

WRITING GROUP GRABBER

Assign each member of your writing group a different book category (picture book, early reader, chapter books, middle grade, and young adult). After reading the book, invite each member to report on subject matter, structure, appeal, and writing style. If possible, share the books with young readers and get their reactions. After reporting on the book, look for reviews of the book and see how members' reports stacked up against the published reviews.

4 GETTING READY TO WRITE

There's nothing between you and the computer screen. You've committed to developing a writing habit, you've set up your tools, and you've narrowed your focus and determined your writing preferences. You are ready to get writing!

Before jumping into it, you'll probably find it valuable to do some planning and make some decisions about the way you plan to tell your story. You will probably change some of these decisions or alter the direction of the story by the time you take it to second or third draft, but having an initial plan in place will keep you focused.

The planning process that you use before beginning your first draft is called prewriting. During the prewriting process, you map out where you need to go. The ultimate goal of prewriting is to do enough homework so that you can move on to a workable first draft. A workable first draft is a draft with enough elements in place that it can be revised instead of discarded. The process of writing then discarding is both frustrating and self-defeating. It stops many writers cold—and they never move ahead into productive writing.

THE BUILDING BLOCKS

There are some key elements you need to consider as you begin the prewriting process. All stories—whether they are for children or adults—have several elements or building blocks in common: character(s), plot, and setting. Each of these building blocks is used in a *unique* way in a children's book, and how you choose to use them will involve deliberate choices on your part.

To understand how these elements are specifically used, let's take a look at a concrete example. In the previous chapter we identified some of the transitions children experience between the ages of four and eight. We also listed some of the relationships that are important to children of those ages. Recall that one of those transitions was starting school and one of the relationships was a sibling relationship. In order to understand technique, let's focus on a story that grows out of that exercise.

Here is the situation: A young girl, whom we will call Emily, is fearful about starting kindergarten. Her brother, Phillip, is in fourth grade and an old hand at school.

WHO IS TELLING THE STORY?

The voice of the story will be determined by who is telling the tale. Many books, especially picture books, have omniscient narrators. An omniscient narrator provides a voice that tells the story. In fact, the omniscient narrator is almost a character in the story itself—with one important distinction—the narrator has nothing at stake in the story. Rather, the omniscient narrator is the storyteller. An omniscient narrator tends to work best in fantasies or fairy tales. If we told Emily's tale through an omniscient voice, it might start something like this:

> In the farthest corner of Mapletown, in a tiny house by the river, lived a young girl named Emily. Emily wasn't afraid of much. She wasn't afraid of big dogs. She wasn't afraid of angry thunderstorms. And she wasn't afraid of the dark woods behind her house.
>
> But she was afraid of one thing—school!

Using an omniscient narrator in this story doesn't quite work. While there is an engaging storytelling feel to the opening, the tone doesn't really convey the intensity of Emily's emotions. And, quite frankly, the story simply sounds contrived and a little silly when told this way.

First Person or Third Person

If we choose not to use an omniscient narrator to tell Emily's story, then we have another choice to make. Do we tell the story in first person or third person? A first-person narrative or first-person viewpoint means that you are writing as if you are the main character, using "I" for the voice in the story. You are, in effect, giving your main character's personal account of the story. Less frequently, a secondary character may give a first-person account of another character's dilemma. First-person narrative has the advantage of creating an immediate sense of intimacy with the reader. It's particularly effective when you are writing for children eight and up because readers this age are attracted to that instant connection with the main characters.

However there is a disadvantage to first-person stories. If you write in first person, it is clear, from the story's outset, that the narrator has survived the crisis in the story. If you need your story to build suspense or tension—especially when it comes to a situation that is life or death—first-person narrative may not be your best choice. By relying on first person, you've basically ruined the suspense because you are telling your reader that the narrating character has survived.

Another disadvantage to first-person stories, especially when writing for younger children, is that the writer needs to adopt the voice and level of sophistication of the narrator. In so doing, the writer may dilute the conflict.

If you choose to write Emily's story in first person, you might start:

> I had never been so scared in my life. And my brother was no help at all!

Third-person narrative is when the writer functions as an outside observer of the events of the plot. To the reader, the writer seems uninvolved with the characters, but behind the scenes, the writer is manipulating the reader through careful use of characterization, plot, and setting.

Third-person narrative is the most natural-sounding narrative technique in children's books, and is the technique that comes most naturally to writers. While readers don't identify as completely with the main character as they might with first person, it does allow the writer a better opportunity to create suspense in the plot, develop secondary characters, and use setting to enhance the story. That's because the writer has the freedom to stray from the main character's voice and viewpoint as he tells the story. If you choose to write Emily's story in third person, it might sound like this:

> Emily had never been so scared in her life. She had hoped that she would be able to rely on Phillip to help her through her first day of school, but he was totally ignoring her.

CHARACTER AND VIEWPOINT

The most important character in any story is the main character—the character who grows and changes as he or she experiences the events in the story. In this case, the main character is Emily. She is the character who is experiencing the conflict of starting school, and she is the one who will experience the most growth and change. She is also the character who needs to show the most emotion in your story.

It is generally not a good idea to have more than one main character, especially in stories for young readers. Developing a number of characters can make your story convoluted and confusing. Also, if you offer a multitude of main characters, your reader might fail to focus on the story or develop empathy with your main character.

You want the reader to connect with your main character in an intimate way. The best way to make that connection is to create a solid identity for your main character. In strong stories, readers empathize with the main character. In fact, in the best stories for children, children feel as if they could even be the main character.

You can create this empathy by using a technique called limited viewpoint, sometimes called limited third-person viewpoint. Limited viewpoint is a version of third person that has the advantage of creating intimacy, but at the same time, preserves the suspense of your story's plot.

When you use limited viewpoint, you closely focus the story around the main character's thoughts and emotions—thereby focusing the reader's attention on the main character. When you write a story through the main character's limited point of view, you only focus on that character's emotions. It's as if you have attached an electrode to that character's brain so that you can see directly through that character's eyes—but you are still telling the story in third person. The feelings of the other characters can be revealed to the reader, but only as the main character or the narrator experiences and relates them to the reader.

Let's return to Emily's dilemma. She is the main character, and so the reader must intimately feel what she is feeling as she starts school. Emily is feeling a sense of excitement, tempered by anxiety and fear. She knows she will miss her mom and her dad. She also knows she is going to an unfamiliar place, and she's worried about getting lost or finding the bathroom.

The character of Phillip may be struggling with his own emotions, but the story isn't focusing on those. That's because Phillip is considered a secondary character. While the reader does not necessarily have to identify with Phillip, it is still helpful for you, as the writer of the story, to know how Phillip feels. Phillip is probably worried about Emily and wants to help her through her anxiety. But there's a problem for Phillip. He is afraid if he seems too helpful to Emily, he will seem uncool to his friends. As the writer of the story, you know this about Phillip, but since he is not the main character, you will not relate this to the reader directly.

In addition to Phillip, Emily also has a mother and father—and their emotions regarding Emily starting school might range from anxiety to relief. Adults' emotions, for the most part, are not actively present in a picture book. The best picture books focus on children as characters, not their adult counterparts, although, again, there are exceptions. Adults are present in picture books, but their emotional lives are usually not at the center of the story.

Back to Emily: She may be able to sense that Phillip is worried. She may also see that Phillip is distancing himself from her. This is Emily's story so she has to relate those emotions to the reader.

How would a narrator do that using limited viewpoint? You might relate her thoughts this way:

Emily couldn't wait to ride the bus with her big brother. When they got on the bus, though, Phillip walked away. Emily watched sadly as he joined his friends, Jack and Mitch, in the back row. She took a seat in the front, right behind the bus driver.

It's probably true that you—as the director of this scene—know intimately what Phillip is feeling. He's feeling guilty. He's feeling pretty comfortable with his friends. He's worried about Emily. You know these things, but Emily doesn't. Since you are telling Emily's story, you can't tell the reader what Phillip is feeling. You can only show those emotions through Emily's eyes. You might do that by writing something like this:

Emily looked back at Phillip. She noticed that he looked at her for just a second and smiled. Then he went back to laughing and talking with his friends.

Now the reader has a sense—through Emily's viewpoint—how Phillip feels. Yet, the story is still firmly Emily's story. Emily is the character that the reader knows and empathizes with, and yet a bit of Phillip's emotions have been revealed without breaking that connection.

Give Them Personality

Good characters are developed through single character viewpoint, but they are also exposed to the reader through their emotions. Character's emotions are most effectively developed when the writer shows those emotions to readers, rather than telling them directly how the character feels. This writing technique is often called "show, don't tell."

To incorporate "show, don't tell" into your own writing, think about how vari-

---

BRING YOUR CHARACTER TO LIFE!

Consider these ways to make your main character distinctive.

1. Give her a name that reflects her personality.
2. Create a handle for your main character. Perhaps the character loves to chew bubble gum or wears purple socks all the time.
3. Let your character speak. Give your character a distinctive way of speaking or a catch phrase she always uses.
4. Mind his mannerisms. Create a character with a mannerism that will allow the reader to identify with him—cracking knuckles, scrunching his forehead, playing with his hair.
5. Be aware of the Name Game. In almost all cases, make sure that your characters' names are easy to pronounce and not too exotic.
6. Vary the names. Make sure that you vary your characters' names so that the reader doesn't confuse them. Using the names Cassie, Kathy, and Katie, for instance, might make it difficult for the reader to distinguish between the names.

ous people around you react in response to their own emotions. You can tell your reader that your main character is nervous, but if you know what mannerisms people use when they are nervous, you can more fully show those emotions to your reader. You might show nervousness by having your character chew her nails or hair, or by giving her a shaky, uncertain voice. As you prepare to write your story, you'll probably find it helpful to make a list of your main character's emotions and how you intend to show those emotions. That way you won't fall into the trap of telling rather than showing.

Whatever way you choose, be aware of clichés. It's too easy to describe a main character as "mad as a hornet" or "green with jealousy." Not only are these comparisons clichés, but they are outside the realm of what children—especially young children—can understand. Work harder at your descriptions. Don't write the first thing that comes into your mind. Rather, search for the better analogy, if you choose to use one. And make sure that you choose a comparison that children can understand.

Make Your Reader Care

Before you commit to your first draft, you'll find it helpful to evaluate your main character to make sure she is sympathetic. The reader of your story needs to care about the main character in a story enough to keep reading. The main character in any story should be imperfect, but these imperfections should not be so exaggerated that the main character becomes unlikable. There is a fine distinction, too, between a character who shows his imperfections and a character who is overly whiny about those imperfections. Readers don't like whiny characters—whether they are in picture books, middle grade books, or even novels for adults.

Also, beware of characters who are too good to be true. Characters should have flaws of some kind so that they are believable and so that the reader can relate to them. Young readers will be particularly drawn to characters who have recognizable flaws or flaws that they share with the readers.

Give Them a Reason

Why does a character do what she does? A character's reasons have to do with motivation. Motivation is essential to the main character's development. It's not enough for a character to want something; you need to tell your reader why the character wants what he wants with the urgency that she does.

The character's motivation also has to make the character worthy. It's not enough, for example, for a character to desire a bicycle just because he wants a bicycle. If that character wants a new bicycle so he can ride to his grandmother's house to spend time with her, then the character's motivation has made his goal worthy and meaningful.

Other Characters

The other characters in your story should also have defined personality traits, but they don't need to be as thoroughly developed as the main character's. Younger readers need to immediately recognize the minor characters and the roles they play in your story, or they can easily become confused. You can do this by developing what I call handles for your minor characters. Perhaps a character always wears purple or pops bubble gum. Bringing that gesture into your story almost every time that character appears can help your reader become oriented to the character and his or her role in the story.

It is helpful, too, when writing for younger children, to create minor characters in a way that feels familiar. A doctor wearing white, a chef with a chef's hat, and a cowboy with a cowboy hat are all images children are familiar with; they will recognize these characters easily and immediately.

PLOT

A plot is a plan of action for what happens in your story. You'll find it easier to get to a workable first draft if you spend some time developing the events of the plot and their sequence. You may choose to do this by writing down the important events of the plot in narrative form. You may also find it helpful to use tools, like a series of note cards, to record the essential events. That way you can rearrange and shuffle the cards to ensure the effectiveness of your plot. Some writers even draw the story out, creating a kind of storyboard for the action that takes place. Whatever method you choose, the goal is to find a way to determine the sequence of events and to ensure that those events fall in logical order and build off each other appropriately.

When it comes to plotting children's books, there are some important things to keep in mind:

- A plot is what keeps your reader reading. Children will put a book down if the plot is not compelling.
- A good plot is logical. The actions in a plot grow naturally from each other.
- A good plot should be believable; it should not depend on coincidence or contrived action.
- A good plot has obstacles that are not easily overcome.

The Conflict and the Climax

In most successful plots, a series of key events happens—each one building on the one before it. In a children's book—as in most fiction—the main character has a problem (known as a conflict) and, through the events of the plot, she solves the problem. Before she resolves the conflict, she will likely come to a place where she feels that the conflict will never be resolved. This is called the *climax*. At the climax, the character should feel as if she is overcoming unbelievable odds to solve the conflict. The climax is the emotional center of the story—the all-or-nothing moment when your character either fails or succeeds.

Because the main character has to struggle to solve the story's conflict, the conflict itself has to be one that challenges the character. The goal should not be easily reached, and the conflict should not be easily resolved. The character should stretch herself to resolve the conflict. And the conflict should be resolved through a series of episodes—at least three—each one building upon the one before it.

The conflict should also be dimensional enough to sustain an entire story. Be sure that you have evaluated your conflict and climax in terms of your character and your character's motivation. Is the conflict something that the main character is likely to care about?

The Resolution

When your main character either succeeds or fails to solve the story's problem, you have reached the story's resolution. Keep in mind that not every character succeeds. Often characters fail, but take away something valuable in the process. They might learn something new, solve a different problem, or come to a new understanding of their situation. Either way, they have been transformed positively by the experience of the events in the plot. And the reader, too, is transformed by the experience.

Your resolution should tie closely with your story's beginning. It should refer back to the conflict that was introduced in the story's opening lines. The main character, having overcome the problem, should reflect on what that accomplishment feels like.

You can tie your story's resolution to its beginnings in a number of different ways. One way is to repeat some of the language or the tone of the story's opening. In my picture book *Whatever I Do, the Monster Does Too!*, the opening begins, "A monster used to live under my bed." After the main character makes three attempts to get rid of the monster, he finally decided that the only way to get rid of the monster is to hug it. When he does that, the monster climbs into bed with him and hugs him back. The last lines of the book tie into those opening lines and effectively resolve the story. "A monster used to live under my bed. Now he lives in my bed, underneath my blankets. When I get really scared, I reach out and hug my monster. And my monster hugs me right back."

The story's resolution should *not* cheat the reader. "It was all a dream" plots rarely work, with some exceptions, the Wizard of Oz story being the most notable. With most "It was all a dream" plots, the reader ends up feeling as if he has been tricked, and he probably won't fully identify with the character growth in the story.

Plot-Building

Let's consider Emily's conflict. She is frightened about starting school. She wants to be comfortable on her first day of kindergarten. What three events, each one building on the one before it, will help her solve her problems?

Episode 1: Conflict is Introduced, and Its Urgency is Developed

Emily's first attempt is to rely on what she knows about school. As she rides the bus, she imagines what school will be like based on what she has heard from Phillip and her older friends. From them, she knows that the school is very large, there are bullies on the playground, and the teachers only let you go to the bathroom when you ask permission. (Notice the emphasis on bathroom. If you know kids, you know that this is a developmentally appropriate preoccupation for a child Emily's age.)

Her first tactic doesn't work—in fact; it makes her even more frightened about starting kindergarten. She has to find another solution to her problem, a solution that is harder to approach than the one she just tried.

Episode 2: Conflict Becomes More Complicated

Emily decides to ask the little girl beside her to relate what kindergarten is like. The girl, who is a year older, gives her some tips, but her portrayal of school society is so exaggerated that it scares Emily even more. The girl suggests that she should have brought two lunches so she can trade with the bullies at lunchtime. She says that it is best to wear pants (Emily has worn a skirt) so that you can do flips on the jungle gym. And the girl also warns about the biggest terror of all—the playground supervisor who has an incredible temper.

Episode 3: The Climax and Resolution

By now, Emily is incredibly anxious. She is so anxious, in fact, that her only choice is to somehow rely on her own inner strength to get her through the day. The problem now is that inner strength isn't enough to get her into the kindergarten building. She knows she has to rely on her inner strength to do something else—something that is extremely difficult for her to do. She has to ask for help from Phillip.

At first blush, it may seem as if Emily isn't really solving the problem on her own. After all, she is turning to Phillip for counsel. But if Emily's character has been developed effectively, the reader knows that asking Phillip for help is difficult task—especially since he seems so reluctant to help her.

How will Phillip respond? His response is important to the plot, but it's not nearly as important as what Emily learns through the process. Perhaps she learns that it's not necessarily a weakness to ask for help. Maybe she learns that her brother's loyalty to her is actually stronger than his loyalty to his friends. If Phillip confesses that he, too, was once frightened about school, she may learn something about her brother's vulnerability. Whatever she learns, Emily must somehow grow and change as a result of the action of the plot.

Plot Points for Middle Grade and Young Adult Novels

Because they are longer and more complex, books for older readers should have plots with more than three episodes, of course. Still, there are three main points in any plot that rise just as the three episodes in pictures and chapter books. If you are plotting a middle grade or young adult novel, you'll want to develop three critical points of dramatic action, each one more intense than the one before it. These critical points should be evenly spaced throughout your narrative so that your plot's timing proceeds effectively.

THE PLOT'S THE THING!

Use this guide to double-check plot effectiveness in your story.

1. Good plots start with a problem. The main character is threatened and responds to that threat.

2. Strong plots look forward not backward. Don't add background information that your reader doesn't need to know. Your reader can figure out the background of the characters from the movement of the plot.

3. Description can add to the plot, but long passages of description slow a plot down.

4. Move the action. Plot starts in the first sentence of your story. The statement of the problem or the threat should start the action. The plot problem should be integrated into every scene and event in the story.

SETTING

The setting is where *and* when your story takes place. Details about your setting can enhance your plot. Keep in mind, however, that your setting needs to grow from a child's perception of the world. Settings should be "kidlike"—playgrounds, schools, backyards, etc. And your description should include details children would recognize vs. details adults would find compelling.

A well-written, sharp description of a setting can bring the story to life for a reader. Remember though that in picture books, the pictures tell half the story. Even in books without pictures, the details of the setting should not dominate the plot or the character development. Instead, those details should be woven into the overall plot.

Keep in mind, too, that a single paragraph in which you describe your setting is not enough. Not only should you integrate the setting into the story, you should ensure that you have revealed the details of the setting through the eyes, ears, and nose of the main character.

Let's return to Emily and her first day at school. The reader will probably know from the illustration that Emily is on a school bus. The reader is also likely to recognize the image of the school when Emily arrives. A large amount of visual description is probably not necessary. In fact, too much visual description is likely to impede the plot.

There are other ways to make the setting come alive through sensory description. Consider smell, for instance. Most of us have a memory of the smell of school bus exhaust. No doubt the smell will only add to Emily's anxiety. You might try a short reference to the sense of smell like this:

> Emily sighed. She smelled the smoky fumes of the school bus. The smell made her head ache.

When she gets to school, the smell may change to that of chalk dust and the smell of the flowers on the teacher's desk. That smell may signal a change in her feeling of anxiety—and may make kindergarten seem much more welcoming than it had previously.

IT TAKES TIME

Effective prewriting and planning takes time. You'll likely be surprised by how much time it takes. Keep in mind, though, that the more time you spend prewriting, the less time you will spend writing a workable draft.

The other positive effect that prewriting has is that it usually makes you anxious to get to the first draft stage. The anxiety you might have felt as you stared at your computer screen or your pad of paper may dissipate as you get to know your characters, your plot, and your setting. It may even seem as if your main character has come to life and is urging you to get started telling her story. (I know Emily is!)

CREATE CHARACTER

The most effective way to create a believable main character is to really get to know the character. Then get to know her further by creating unique traits and characteristics.

Use the worksheet below to develop the character traits for a character in a book you are working on.

Character's name:

Gender:

Physical characteristics:

Age and grade level:

Hair color:

Eye color:

Size:

Other physical traits:

Name three things your main character is good at:

Name three things your main character is not good at:

Who is in your main character's family?

Where does your main character live? What are the details of his room? His house?

What four emotions dominate your main character? How does she show her reaction to these emotions?

"WHAT IF . . ."

Now that you have completed the worksheet about your character, consider some "what if" possibilities.

What if your main character had to move to a new town or school?

What if your main character lived in a very remote location?

What if your main character had supernatural abilities?

Add your own "what ifs" here:

CREATIVE WAYS TO GET TO CHARACTER

Write a letter from your main character to you, as if you are pen pals. I've included one from the character of Emily to me.

> Dear Tracey,
>
> My mom is writing the words down to this letter as I say them because I can't write yet. But I will learn soon! I am going to start kindergarten next week. I'm really, really scared. I have to take a big school bus. Then I have to find my room and everything. I am glad Phillip is along to help me.
> Love,
> Emily

Interview your main character. Ask him about his motivation, his goals, his likes and dislikes. Question him about certain mannerisms that he has and use those mannerisms to get to the heart of his emotions. Write the questions you are going to ask below. Here are some examples:

> What is your favorite thing to do?
>
> Why do you keep bouncing that basketball?
>
> What kinds of grades do you get in school?

OTHER WAYS TO GET TO KNOW YOUR CHARACTER

Write several diary entries in your main character's voice. Try focusing three entries around the three major plot events you have in mind.

Cut out a picture from a magazine or newspaper of what you imagine your main character looks like.

Draw a sketch of your main character.

Draw a picture of something as if you are your main character.

If your main character is school age, make a report card for your main character.

Write out your main character's daily—or weekly—schedule.

Write a description of your main character from another character's viewpoint. (Write a description of Emily from Phillip's viewpoint, for instance.)

Make lists of your main character's favorite things: books, color, foods, etc.

THE POWER OF THREE

Choose one of the "what if" questions from the exercise above, and then write the three corresponding episodes in the plot that build to resolution. I've included examples from the Emily story, but you should use your own plot to develop these episodes.

Episode 1: Emily

> Emily tries to impress upon her new stepbrother that she knows all about
> school and what it takes to get through the first day of kindergarten. In so
> doing, she tries to convince herself as well.

Episode 1: Your story

Episode 2: Emily

> Emily confidently strolls into school and ends up in the 6th grade class, in-
> stead of in kindergarten.

Episode 2: Your story

Episode #3 (the climax): Emily

> Emily breaks down and asks Phillip for help, even though the two have been
> fighting since they moved in together.

Episode 3 (the climax): Your story

PICK A CLASSIC

Consider these classic children's tales and determine what three or four episodes build upon each other to make up the plot.

> *The Three Little Pigs*
> *The Little Engine that Could*
> *The Little Red Hen*
> *Goldilocks and the Three Bears*

Now identify the climax and the story's resolution.

SET IT RIGHT!

Consider the following settings. Indicate how you would use all five senses to describe the scene. Make sure that you consider what a child would notice, rather than imposing an adult perspective. I've started the first one for you.

Beach

Touch: sand, cold water

Hear: seagulls, rush of water

Taste: taste of cold lemonade character is drinking

Sight: blue skies, blue water, little contrast between the two

Smell: fish mingled with suntan lotion

Snowy day

Stormy night

Inside a library

Amusement park

Shopping mall

Grandparents' kitchen

KIDSTUFF

Consider the following situations. How would a child's reaction differ from an adult? An example has been included.

Parents are getting divorced.

Adult reaction: Sadness and anger

Child reaction: Self-involved concern: Where will I live? Who will take care of me?

Pet dies.

Adult reaction:

Child reaction:

Best friend moves away.

Adult reaction:

Child reaction:

Grandmother comes to live with family.

Adult reaction:

Child reaction:

 WRITING GROUP GRABBER

Invite each writing group member to write a sensory description of a setting without giving away the name of the setting. See if members of the group can determine what the setting is from the sensory details alone.

5 THE WORKABLE DRAFT

So far, we've developed ideas for stories and learned about the essential building blocks of fiction. At the same time, we've developed ways to prewrite so that you are ready to write your story. Now we are going to consider what you need to do to bring it all together in a workable first draft.

WHAT IS A WORKABLE DRAFT?

For most writers, a workable first draft is an integrated version of various prewriting activities. A first draft is still just that—a first draft—but it's somewhat more developed than a simple plot, character, and setting sketch. As discussed in the last chapter, an important rule of thumb about a first draft is that there must be enough in that first draft to revise and refine. Characters need to be developed enough so that you can evaluate them and give them more consistency and depth if you need to. The plot needs to have a kind of logic and rhythm to it, even if you end up refining it. And the setting should be defined and fairly well-balanced with the plot.

A workable first draft means you are making progress. There will be revision to be sure—extensive revision, most likely—but if you rely on your prewriting activities and your predraft planning, you will likely not have to stop and reinvent your story from scratch. That start-all-over mentality can cause serious frustration and stop you from ever reaching your goal.

During the workable first draft stage, it is essential that you shut out your inner critic or any outside evaluations. Resist the urge to stop midway through and evaluate what you've done. And resist the urge to pick up the phone, call a member of your writing group, and read a passage. Wait until you are finished to engage in these kinds of activities; if done too early, they are likely to be self-defeating.

While the workable first draft should have all the important events and elements of your story in it, it does not have to be perfect in terms of grammar, spelling, and the like. Ignore those technical details for now. They will be important in a later stage of revision.

In order to craft this workable first draft, let's consider the parts of your story: the opening, where the conflict is introduced; the body (often called the middle), where you develop the story's episodes; and the ending where the conflict is brought to a conclusion.

Your Opening

The beginning of your book should grab the reader and make him want to keep reading. To do this, you'll need to introduce your story's subject and conflict in the first sentence or paragraph if you can. As you craft your story's opening, consider how to create a sense of urgency. You want your reader (and the editor who is considering your story) to be *hungry* for the rest of the story. As you develop your opening, be careful not to focus too heavily on character description or setting description. In your opening, your reader does not need to know how old your main character is, what she looks like, or where she lives. Those details will become apparent later on in the story. Instead, get to the heart of the story's problem.

You should also introduce the story's problem in a way that makes it matter to the reader. Your opening should be able to pass the "so what?" test. If the story doesn't matter to the reader, he won't keep reading. Just as important, if the story's opening isn't compelling, an editor won't get past the first page of your submission.

Consider the story from the last chapter about Emily and the first day of school. In order to draw the reader into the story, you could start with:

> Emily tried to hold her hand steady on her backpack straps. She didn't want to admit to anyone what she was feeling. She would only admit it to herself. *I am scared. Really, really scared.*
>
> Emily had thought she would be excited about starting kindergarten, but instead, her palms were sweaty, she had goosebumps on her arms, and she couldn't stop feeling as if she had forgotten something.

With this opening, we've established both Emily's point of view and the immediate problem that is driving the story. The reader immediately feels empathy for Emily and will be compelled to keep reading to determine how Emily solves her problem.

Notice, too, how the language used appeals to children. The adjectives "really, really" would probably not be appropriate in a story for adults. But repetition of these adjectives gives the story the feel of a child's voice, even though they are only used as part of Emily's thought process in the story.

Notice one other important feature of this opening: It started with Emily, the main character in the story. The story would not have been nearly as effective if it began with:

"Climb on board," the bus driver barked to Emily.

Starting with Emily's conflict and her reaction pulls your reader in more thoroughly.

THE BODY

The body, or middle part of your story, should focus on the three to four episodes you've developed that will allow the main character to solve her problem. Each episode should build in intensity so that the solution seems more and more difficult to achieve. The last episode should be the most dramatic and should suggest to the reader that the main character may, in fact, fail to meet her goal.

As you develop the middle episodes in your story, make sure that the episodes build appropriately. In first draft stage, many writers put the most dramatic episode in the story first rather than at the end.

The body of your story should also be compelling enough to keep readers engaged. If you are writing a picture book, this is particularly important. Youngsters have short attention spans. They will become bored easily, unless you give them a reason to be caught up in the suspense of page-turning. The best picture books make children breathless to turn the next page to discover the next surprise that is waiting for them.

If you are writing for middle grade and young adult readers, the body of your story should be more intricate. You can spend more time developing characters, using plot twists, and moving from setting to setting. In fact, the interplay of the building blocks in middle grade and young adult books is part of their appeal. The reader keeps reading in part because he wants to see how everything fits together in the plot's conclusion.

As you build a more intricate plot for older readers, though, remember your three plot points. What are the three points of dramatic action that are key to the character growth and plot resolution? You may want to write them down on index cards and keep them handy in case your plot starts getting out of hand.

THE CONCLUSION

The conclusion of your story should reiterate the solution to the story's problem but just as importantly, it should emphasize the character growth that has occurred along the way. That character growth has to be lightly stated. It's easy to get heavy-handed at the end of a story, especially if you are trying to demonstrate a strong moral or lesson. But your reader should be able to get the message without you having to spell it out precisely for him.

Remember that your main character doesn't always have to attain the goal she aspired to in the beginning of the book. If she doesn't achieve that intended goal, she has to achieve something else: She needs to have learned something or gained a new insight. Whatever she attains, make sure that you lay this out for the reader directly.

Keep in mind, too, that your main character should be firmly in control of your story's conclusion. She needs to solve the problem herself, and this needs to be firmly stated in the story's resolution. At some point in the conclusion, the main character should reflect on what has happened and what she has learned in the process.

The conclusion of your story, particularly if it is a picture book, should tie in with your story's beginning. Good picture books are like a full circle. The beginning and ending are integrated fully with each other.

THE FORCE OF YOUR MAIN CHARACTER

As you develop your workable first draft, make sure that your main character is the major force in the story. The main character needs to be in every scene of the story, but, more importantly, he needs to be acting and reacting in every scene. Don't let minor characters run away with your story line.

You will also want to make sure that you reveal your character bit by bit to your reader. Readers want to discover this character on their own. They want to get to know a main character much as they do a new friend. Be sure that you don't throw too much character detail in too soon.

Another element that you will want to nail down during the workable first draft stage is your character's motivation. That motivation needs to be consistent throughout your entire plot. The reason your character wants something in the story's beginning should be the same reason in the middle and the end.

DIALOGUE

In order to really know your characters, especially your main character, your reader needs to hear them speak. This is why dialogue is so important. While there are many notable stories that do not use dialogue, most stories incorporate dialogue into the story's structure.

Integrating dialogue into your story effectively is one of the things an editor will be looking for as she reads your story. Effective use of dialogue sets serious writers apart from more amateurish ones.

Dialogue should be more than just conversation in a story. It should reveal information about your character and move the plot along in significant ways. If dialogue doesn't move the plot along, it does not belong in the story. If dialogue doesn't sound natural, it doesn't reveal any important information about your character.

Keep in mind that dialogue can break grammatical conventions. It can contain sentence fragments, grammatical mistakes, and slang and jargon, as long as that's how your character speaks and it can be understood by the reader.

Passages that express what your main character is thinking or doing should be interspersed among dialogue. Remember to let your main character think by reflecting on what has happened or on what has been said. Your characters should also react as real people do to conversation—with gestures, facial expressions, and mannerisms. Long passages of dialogue fail to keep your readers' attention and slow your plot down.

Internal Dialogue

Internal dialogue is dialogue that your main character hears in his head—what he thinks. It's important for readers to hear what a main character is thinking. There's a level of intimacy that is revealed in internal dialogue that contributes to the reader's empathy with the main character.

Internal dialogue should be used by your main character only. Your workable first draft should strive for a balance between internal dialogue, actual dialogue, and the narrative itself.

INTERNAL DIALOGUE

Use internal dialogue to:

- Intensify your main character's emotions.
- Create a sense of intimacy with your main character and your reader.
- To show an emotion that a main character has that he has not shared with the other characters in the story.
- Vary your narrative. Feelings can be described and stated through first-person internal dialogue.

VOCABULARY AND READABILITY

As you develop your draft, you may be concerned about reading level and vocabulary. Unless you are writing for an educational publisher that requires books to be at precisely the right reading level, you can probably relax. Most often, difficult words can be understood in the context of the story or novel. In fact, using higher-level words—particularly if they sound interesting—is a great way to engage children and to help them expand their vocabulary.

Consider the word *chartreuse* for example. Most children of picture-book age would not know that chartreuse means yellow green. With very little explanation, however, they will understand it in context, especially if they read it in a passage like this one: "Spring was breaking through the snow in the mountains. Tiny chartreuse leaves were appearing from the buds on the trees."

WORD CHOICE

While you don't need to be overly concerned with readability, you should still consider word choice in the workable first draft stage. In everyday speech, we use general adjectives all the time. We say it's a beautiful day, for example, rather than explaining specifically, how the day is beautiful. You can enliven your writing and create more vivid word pictures if you select the most specific adjective you can find. Rather than use general adjectives, stretch yourself to find more precise, interesting words. Search not only for the *right* word, but the *best* word to express what you are trying to say.

One way to ensure that you have used vivid word choice is to apply the rule of five senses. Think about how the five senses can be used to vividly develop the scene at hand.

REPETITION AND PATTERNED PHRASES

One way that you can reinforce the reading skills of your audience is to use repetition and patterned phrases throughout your story. Prereaders, especially, will pick up on the phrases and begin to anticipate and predict them in your book.

My picture book *Annabelle's Awful Waffle* relied on this device. In it, Annabelle is piling her waffle with all sorts of crazy ingredients. Why? Because she wants to make it "awful." No matter what she adds to it, the waffle does not become as awful as she wants it to be. In the book, I use the phrase, "But that waffle wasn't awful enough yet" as a kind of refrain throughout. Children, especially children who are just beginning to read, will learn to predict that phrase and repeat it as part of the story.

FINDING A TITLE

In workable first draft stage, it is a good idea to title your story if you haven't done so already. Titles have a way of creating an identity for your story. You may change the title later on—or your publisher may do so for you—but your title in workable first draft stage will help you reinforce the idea that you know the essence of your story.

While we often judge books by their covers, we just as often judge books by their titles. Intriguing titles not only pique a child's interest, but they will make an editor curious as well.

There are three requirements for a good title:

- A good title makes the reader want to read the story.
- A good title doesn't give away the story's ending.
- A good title reflects what the story is about.

Consider the title of Dr. Seuss's classic, *And to Think That I Saw It on Mulberry Street*. Readers are attracted to that title because they want to know just what it was that was seen on Mulberry Street. The title to Paula Danziger's chapter book *Amber Brown is Not a Crayon* features clever wordplay that draws the reader to the story. *Annabelle's Awful Waffle* uses rhyme and alliteration to attract the reader.

As you work on the perfect title, it's important to think visually once again. What visual images do the titles you are considering evoke? What can you imagine will be the main focus on the cover?

Keep in mind, however, that no matter how great your title is—and how wonderful the visual imagery you connect to it is—the selection of the final title and cover image is always up to the publishing company.

THE TITLE TEST

Does your title:

- Capture the essence of the story?
- Develop a sense of suspense?
- Use clever or descriptive word choice?
- Suggest an illustration?
- Conceal the story's ending?
- Give an indication of who the characters are?
- Give an indication of what the conflict might be?

GETTING STARTED WITH A BANG

Rewrite the following passages so that the story's conflict is in the first line of the story.

1. Emily walked down the sidewalk toward the school bus. It was a crisp fall day and the sun was shining. Somehow, though, Emily didn't feel like smiling. She was too scared.

2. Pumpkin was an orange calico cat with one white spot over his right eye. He mewed softly as Katie rubbed his back. He snuggled up into Katie's arms. *I've got to find a way to keep him*, Katie said to herself.

3. "Put down your pencils, class," the teacher said. Twenty-five third graders put down their pencils and looked at the front of the room. The wind rustled the leaves outside the school window. Sam was sure he hadn't passed the math quiz. And if he didn't pass the math quiz, he wouldn't be able to play baseball that spring.

4. The snow was falling harder, covering the trees in a cuddly white blanket. Two stars twinkled above the mountain. The moon was just beginning to rise. Robert shuddered in the cold. *How had he gotten so lost?* he wondered.

NEW GOALS

In the exercises below, each character does not attain what he or she wants. What alternative goal or piece of knowledge might each character attain instead of the original one?

1. Sarah wants a bicycle so she can visit her grandmother across town. She doesn't get the bicycle at the end of the story. What does she attain that will help her visit her grandmother?

2. Sam wants to stop his family from moving to Texas because he is afraid of losing his best friend. He cannot stop his family from moving. What can he do to ensure that he will still have a best friend?

3. Jennifer wants a kitten because she loves cats. Her little brother is allergic to cats, and her parents tell her she cannot have one. Since she can't have a kitten, what does Jennifer do to experience being around her favorite kind of pet?

LET'S TALK!

Write a dialogue between:

Cinderella and Prince Charming as they are dancing

Snow White and Little Red Riding Hood after they meet in the woods

Jack from *Jack in the Beanstalk* giving advice to the three little pigs

Goldilocks and Rapunzel discussing hair styles

A little girl talking to a kitten

A boy talking to his coach after he loses a game

INTERNAL DIALOGUE

Rework the phrases below so that they express the same sentiment in internal dialogue rather than through narrative:

Jennifer wanted a cat more than ever.

I just have to have a kitten, Jennifer said to herself.

Phillip couldn't find his favorite shirt.

Megan hated cutting the grass.

Peter wanted the shiny new bike.

David was afraid to dive off the board.

GENERALLY SPEAKING

Identify the general adjectives below and replace them with adjectives that are more precise or descriptive

The teacher was nice.

The storm was scary.

Sally has pretty hair.

Sam was feeling very sad.

Terry got a brand new bicycle.

COLOR YOUR ADJECTIVES AND VERBS

To ensure that you are using unique and vivid descriptions, come up with alternatives for the following colors:

Yellow: Lemon

Red

Green

Blue

Black

Now come up with alternatives to the following verbs:

Fall: Topple

Run

Fly

Walk

Eat

TITLES

Retitle the following classic tales:

David and Goliath: Why the Giant Fell

The Tortoise and the Hare

Three Billy Goats Gruff

Aladdin and the Magic Lamp

The Boy Who Cried Wolf

The Little Match Girl

 WRITING GROUP GRABBER

Select an untitled manuscript that your writers group is reviewing. After reviewing the story, each member of the group should write down a prospective title. Evaluate each title in terms of:

Appropriateness

Interest

Word Choice

Brevity

Creating a desire on the part of the reader and editor to read the story.

6 THREE ROUNDS OF REVISION

One of my favorite writers, James Thurber, once said, "I am not a writer. I am a rewriter." What Thurber suggests is that the real work of writing is revision. Your workable first draft needs reworking, rethinking, and rebuilding before it is ready to send off to a publisher.

Some writers revise as they go along, reworking plot, sequence, and dialogue until the draft they create is almost final. The most effective rewriting, however, is done after the *entire* draft is completed, from beginning to end. Then you can see how the story shapes up, where it is logical and where it isn't, where it builds effectively and where it falls flat.

Realistically, there are *more* than three rounds of revision required for any one manuscript. There are, however, three specific phases of the revision process. The first phase involves looking at big picture issues. The second revision phase focuses more closely on the big picture issues you identified in round one; it should feel as if you are looking at your manuscript through a zoom lens. Then there's round three. That's where you take a microscope to your manuscript, examining every element and correcting any grammar, punctuation, and spelling mistakes.

TAKE A BREATHER

The first rule of first draft revision: Don't do it right away. Take a little time to celebrate first. Congratulate yourself on the fact that you have completed your story. Then let your draft rest as long as you can let it. Move on to another piece of writing or to some research you've been longing to do. Read your favorite children's book again and see if you see it through different eyes now that you've joined the ranks of children's writers yourself.

The main point of taking a breather is that you'll return to your first draft with a new perspective. You'll be better prepared to evaluate the draft as objectively as possible.

GO IT ALONE

You may be tempted to ask your writers group or a friend or mentor to help you determine the appropriate revisions. Resist this temptation. In almost all cases, the first draft should be for your eyes only. Only when you are confident that you have developed the draft to the best of your ability—working through it several times— should you ask for the input of others. If you go out to the public with a first draft too soon, you risk becoming demoralized by criticism.

You also risk wasting your critiquer's time. It's respectful to ask for a second opinion only after you have gotten your manuscript into the best shape possible.

ROUND ONE

As I mentioned above, your first evaluation of your draft should look at big picture issues. In first draft revision, you're not looking at the nitty-gritty details. Punctuation, grammar, and spelling should be ignored for now. What you are looking for is the essence of your story and whether you have communicated that essence effectively.

One effective way to get to the essence of your story is to try and paraphrase it. Can you state what your story is about in one or two sentences? If not, it's likely that your story went offtrack somewhere. The plot became too complicated, the characters ran away with the story, or the setting overshadowed what was really going on.

Overwriting/Underwriting

If you do a careful analysis of your first draft, you will likely discover that you have overwritten some elements. Writing experts have estimated that every first draft can be cut by 10 percent. Your story likely fits within this category. Look for places in your story where there is fat—where you have overwritten. Cut these. Character and setting descriptions are typically overdone in a first draft. (This is completely logical, after all. You, as the writer, are trying to get to know these elements of your story.) Recognize that you won't lose these sections forever. Later, you may rewrite them with meatier passages that more directly support your story and its purpose.

You have probably underwritten other elements. First draft problems usually involve characters who are developed without specific detail, a climax that is not dramatic enough, or a viewpoint that is not as tightly controlled as it needs to be.

There may also be a few red herrings in your first draft. Red herrings can include ideas you introduced that went nowhere, characters whom once seemed important but are now dispensable, or elements of the setting that just seem out of place. You need to weed out as much of them as possible in first round revision.

Does It Sing?

Reading your story to an empty room—and actually listening to it—can be an important step in the first draft revision process. Picture books, especially, are meant to be read aloud. In fact, good picture books pass the "read-aloud" test when children ask for the same book to be read aloud again and again.

Tape recording yourself reading your story is another way to figure out how to streamline your first draft. Good stories for children are like wonderful music. The words and phraseology should have a lyrical rhythm.

Another way to see if your story passes the read aloud test is to ask a colleague to read it aloud for you. Hearing your story through a different voice can be an enlightening experience. Note where your reader picks up the rhythm or misses it completely. Do the humorous passages work? Does the entire book flow the way it should?

When you read your work aloud or hear it read aloud, you are likely to notice awkward and convoluted sentences. Wherever your tongue trips up, your reader's eyes will trip up. These sentences or passages should be rewritten for clarity.

You will also notice repetition of words and phrases when your manuscript is read out loud. Unless this has been done for effect, you should revise your manuscript so it doesn't repeat itself.

Finally, you will no doubt discover very long sentences that need to be brought down to size. When reading your work aloud, take note of wherever you need to take a breath. You should end such sentences earlier or add punctuation so that your reader gets a breather as well.

Does It Make Sense?

Another issue you need to attend to in first draft revision is the logic of your story. Children's stories are full of surprises, of course, but there is a predictability to them. The predictable nature has something to do with what is called a happy ending. Young readers, especially of picture book age, expect that the story's problem will eventually become resolved. *How* it is resolved is the heart of the story. Not resolving a story properly or introducing an additional plot problem that comes from nowhere will confuse and frustrate your reader.

During your first draft revision, you'll also want to check for consistency. You may have changed your mind about certain characters, the flow of your plot, and which details of your setting to emphasize. Make sure that when you have made changes that these changes are consistent throughout the entire manuscript.

Is It Responsible?

You are writing for an impressionable audience. While you want to avoid talking down to your reader, you do want to make sure you are writing responsible literature, and the best time to do this reality check is in first round revision. Think back to *Alice's Adventures in Wonderland*. Recall when Alice drank the liquid that made her shrink. That could potentially be a dangerous suggestion for a young child. (Because the Alice story is so obviously a fantasy, however, it probably passes the responsibility test. The same is true of the most wonderful episodes in the Harry Potter series, episodes that may seem irresponsible at first read.)

Just as important is the way you develop your adult characters in your story. They should react in responsible ways. If a child turns to them for help, they should offer that help, although they should never be central to the book's resolution. That is up to the child main character.

Remember, this: Cut or rewrite any passage in your story that could cause kids to endanger themselves or to act inappropriately.

No Grown-Ups Allowed

At the same time that you are ensuring that your adult characters are responsible, you need to keep their interference in the plot to a minimum. Often, stories that get into trouble in first draft do so because the grown-up character or the grown-up voice is too central to the story. That's a logical mistake. Children's book writers *are* grown-ups. It's difficult to stop ourselves from imposing our views on the story. If you find yourself having difficulty, especially with plot development, try redrafting the story without the grown-ups. You can always bring them back later.

Description

Your story likely includes some passages of description of the setting or the character. When you revise your manuscript, you'll want to make sure that your description is as sharp as it can be. You'll also want to make sure that you haven't overdescribed something. Too much description can slow down your plot. Using a highlighter or pen, go through your manuscript and underline every passage of description and every adjective and adverb. See if you can part with 25 percent of the descriptive passages in the story. If you are writing a book that is illustrated, such cuts can be even more critical since the illustrations do much of the visual work of the story.

Does It Matter?

The most important and final question you need to ask yourself about your first draft: Does it really matter? Will the young reader care enough about the plot and the characters to take something away from the story? Will the adult—who is presumably reading the story aloud if it is a picture book—see a quality or feel a message as a result of reading the story?

It's a subtle difference, but there are many, many stories out there that are simply not big enough to be picture books. They work fine as stories in children's magazines, but there isn't enough meat for a thirty-two-page book. The stories matter—they just don't matter enough to be a book.

To get a sense of what makes for a good story vs. a good book, compare your favorite picture book to a story from one of the many fine children's magazines, such as *Cricket*. What differences do you see?

THE DUMMY

All children's books require revision in the areas described here, but if you are writing a picture book, you'll need to take an extra step. This is because you won't really know if your story works as a picture book until you actually lay it out like a picture book. The best way to do that is to actually make a "dummy" picture book. A dummy is really no more than a pretend book in which you position your story. When you make a dummy, you'll be looking to see if there are enough scenes to illustrate, the pacing is right, and the right words fall in the right places in the book.

There are several ways to make a dummy, but the best way is to make a pretend book out of simple 8½″ × 11″ paper. Simply take eight pieces of paper, fold them in half at the middle, and assemble a little book. You may want to staple the spine of the book (the fold) for ease of use.

Now you have what is essentially thirty-two pages. Not all of the pages will contain your story however. You'll need to allow space for front matter in your dummy. Front matter generally consists of a title page and a copyright page. The dedication may appear on the copyright page or it can appear on a page of its own. Your front matter, then, will take up either page one and two, or pages one, two, and three.

The decision regarding how many pages your front matter takes up isn't simply a matter of preference. It is a strategic decision that depends on whether you want to start you book on page three, a single-page spread, or on page four, which is a double-page spread. A single-page spread is one page that shows story and illustration. A double-page spread consists of two facing pages and a single illustration that spans the center (called the gutter) of the book. Double-page spreads have the advantage of allowing for larger, more detailed illustrations. Double-page spreads also slow the rhythm of your story, allowing your reader a rest within the plot. Single-page spreads contain an illustration that fits on a single page; this single illustration can feel more intimate to the reader and offer a kind of close-up view.

Deciding whether to start on a single- or double-page spread also has to do with the concept of page turning. If your story begins with a question, if you want to add suspense after the opening scene, or if there is a kind of "wow" factor in the beginning of your story, you'll want to consider starting on a single page for faster pacing.

At this point, it's time to play with your story to see if it works. Printing the story several times and then cutting it up and positioning text on the page is one good way to give your story a picture book test. To help determine where page breaks occur, look for scene changes or changes in the action of the characters. If that doesn't work, read the story out loud. Introduce a page break where you have natural pauses in the rhythm of your reading.

When you do this, you will likely discover problems with your story that were not immediately apparent when you wrote it. You will probably pinpoint weak transitions, wordiness, or explanations that aren't thorough enough. You may find that you have too much action in certain parts of the story and not enough in others. You may even find that you have created passages that just can't be illustrated effectively.

Then you must go back and revise to overcome some of these problems. Then do another dummy, if you feel you need to.

Once you have your story to the point that you think the pacing works, try and imagine what illustrations might appear on each page. Now you are evaluating the book's visual appeal and pacing. Ask yourself these questions:

- Is there too much visual action on any particular page? Not enough?
- Are there too many scene changes? Not enough?
- Does the image and text on one page draw you to turn to the next page?
- Does each scene on each page move the story forward?
- Does the story flow well? Are there transitions to orient the reader to each new scene?
- Are there the right number of words on each page? (In general, there should be enough words so that the passage can be read in the time it takes a reader to take in the illustration.)

It's likely that you will reevaluate your story based on what you discover through the dummy process. You may go back, rewrite, and then re-dummy.

It's important to note here that the dummy is only an early revision tool. It's not something publishers expect to receive—especially if it is as amateurish as the one I've explained here. If you are an illustrator, there are rare occasions when sending a dummy may be helpful, but in general, publishers are much more impressed by a cleanly typed, straightforward manuscript with no illustrations included.

When should you work through a dummy? Some writers like to test their ideas via dummies as a step to the second draft. They may return to the dummy process again later on—especially if they make significant changes through the various drafts of their story. Other writers may find it more valuable to dummy their book at next-to-final draft stage. Whichever way you choose, make sure you test your story this way to determine whether you really have created a picture book, with all the narrative and visual episodes that good picture books have.

ON TO ROUND TWO!

After you've completed the big picture revision of the story, it's time for round two. In round two, you are looking for the "smaller" big problems with the story. It's as if you've clicked your editorial camera to its closest setting, honing in on some of the finer details. You may be noticing some problems with grammar, punctuation, and spelling at this stage. If you are fairly certain the draft is going the way you want it to go, it's okay to begin correcting them now. If you feel there is substantial rewriting still to be done, it's best to hold off on the technical matters. You may end up rewriting entire passages, and you will still need to correct those passages anyway.

Plot Check One More Time

Second round revision should involve one more close check of your plot. At the risk of being repetitious, review the plot, looking again for an opening that grabs the reader, three or four key events that build in intensity, and a resolution that focuses on character development. Make sure, too, that you identify any plot stoppers—extraneous details that slow your plot down. These might be unnecessary narrative passages, dialogue that doesn't move the plot forward, or descriptions of settings that stop the plot cold. Look at every sentence, every phrase, every detail, and ask yourself: How important is this detail in moving the plot forward?

Soft Resolutions

Double-check your resolution one more time to make sure the ending of your story is effective. In first round revision, the story's ending may not have gotten the adequate attention it needs. Make sure your ending isn't a throwaway ending. Look at your resolution and determine whether you've hit your reader over the head with a lesson or a moral. If you have done that, it's time to rework the ending and soften it a little. Finally, if your story is complex emotionally, make sure your ending is hopeful. Not all stories have to end happily, but children do deserve hopeful endings.

Transitions

As you scrutinize your plot one more time, you'll also want to make sure you have adequate transitions in your story. Transitions are like bridges that connect the parts of your story together. They orient the reader in terms of time and space, which is especially important for young readers. Look for places where time has passed, and make sure you use phrases that indicate the passage of time like, "the next day," "after school," or "by that afternoon." To indicate when your character has moved from place to place, use references to your setting. If your character has moved from her classroom to the playground, for instance, you don't need to narrate every step of her passage. You can do this simply by making reference to where she is:

> Emily ran out the door of her classroom and sat under the big tree on the playground.

Character, Again

Second round revision should offer a double check on characters as well. Look one more time and make sure that your main character solves the story's problem on his own. Your main character can get help, but he should be in charge of his own problem and the problem's solution. If you are tightly controlling point of view, your main character should also be in every scene in the story. And remember that your reader needs to be inside your main character's head. The reader needs to feel empathy for that character.

You'll also want to carefully read your story to make sure you have consistently described and developed your characters. This is especially true of secondary and minor characters, characters that you probably haven't paid as much attention to. Characters should appear the same way in every scene; a character who has blonde hair on page one should not be a brunette on page four. If a character fusses with his glasses on page two, he should still have glasses on page five. If a character displays a certain trait, that trait should always be attributed to the same character.

POINT OF VIEW CHECKLIST

1. Is your main character in every scene in the story?
2. Identify places where you reveal your main character's emotions. Does your story do this frequently enough for your reader to identify with her?
3. Check that you haven't allowed another character's emotions to drive the story. Make sure that when you have revealed another character's emotions, you have done so through your main character's perspective.

Show, Don't Tell

In this round of revision, you'll want to pay close attention to passages in which you've told the reader something, rather than showing it to the through the action of the plot. There will always be some telling in every story, of course, but the best fiction for children relies more on showing. Look at every adjective that you have included in your story. Do you really need that adjective, or can you show your reader what you mean through action instead?

Tense

Most stories for children are told in past tense, not present. Past tense sounds more natural and lends itself better to storytelling. Whichever tense you choose, make sure you are consistent throughout your entire story. A common problem in early drafts is the tendency to switch back and forth, especially if you have used large passages of internal dialogue.

Passive and Active Voice

While it is important to vary the sentence structure in your story, it is just as important to acknowledge that active voice is preferred to passive voice. As you complete round two of your revision, take a hard look at any sentences in your story that use passive voice and consider recasting them using active voice. Ask yourself which is better:

Passive:

The frightened feelings Emily had were left behind.

or

Active:

Emily left behind the frightened feelings she had.

Dialogue

Handling dialogue effectively can be one of the most difficult fine points to master. Check again that the dialogue moves the plot forward. It should also have the rhythm of real speech; it shouldn't sound awkward, stiff, or formal. If you are fairly confident that your passages of dialogue are effectively positioned in your second draft, you can start to fine-tune that dialogue to make it natural and effective.

Identifying Your Speaker

Tag lines, sometimes called dialogue attributors, are used to identify the speaker of dialogue. These tag lines are nothing more than the "he said" or "she said" that occurs before or after a passage of speech. In fiction that is aimed at adults, tag lines can be minimized. Young readers, though, need to be told more clearly who is saying what.

You don't always have to use a tag line to identify your reader. There are other ways to indicate the speaker to the reader. Consider this phrase:

Emily cleared her throat. "I'm scared."

In this phrase, it's clear that Emily is speaking. You don't need a tag line. The reader probably already knows that she is scared from the subsequent description in the book. Plus she cleared her throat, a good indication that she intended to speak.

Many writers struggle with the monotony of the standard "he/she said" tag. They try to vary the verb that describes speech. Or they add an adjective to help relieve what seems to be a repetitive, monotonous phrase.

The fact is—there is nothing wrong with "he said" or "she said." Dialogue that stretches the point by using outlandish phrases, verbs, or adjectives to describe what is being said does not sound genuine. In fact, it can sound downright ridiculous.

You may choose to vary your tag line occasionally, but make sure that you do it for effect. If you use an alternative to *said* every time your character speaks, you will dilute the overall effect.

If you do choose to occasionally vary from *said*, make sure that you use dialogue attribution that actually describes speaking. The phrase:

"That's so funny," Phillip laughed.

simply doesn't work. People don't laugh and talk at the same time.

Just as people don't laugh entire phrases, they do not speak in unison. The response in the following exchange isn't believable:

"Can you come to my party?" Emily asked.
"Oh yes," Sally and Jennie said.

Rewriting the passage this way makes it sound more natural:

"Can you come to my party?" Emily asked.
"Oh yes," Sally said. Jennie nodded in agreement.

It's also perfectly acceptable to break up a passage of dialogue with a gesture or other action. Consider this phrase:

"I don't want to go to school today, tomorrow, or ever because I'm so scared," Emily said.

This long phrase might be more effective this way:

"I don't want to go to school today, tomorrow, or ever," Emily said, stopping to catch her breath, "because I'm so scared."

Note that because Emily is reciting what is really a full sentence, commas are used to indicate the slight interruption. If she were actually saying two sentences, a preferred punctuation would be:

"I don't want to go to school today, tomorrow or ever," Emily said, stopping to catch her breath. "I don't want to go to school because I'm so scared."

Other Fine Points of Dialogue

Not knowing the fine points of dialogue marks you as an amateur to the editor reading your work. Dialogue that is incorrectly handled or punctuated tells the editor that the writer doesn't pay attention to such details and doesn't pay attention to dialogue conventions when he reads (or, worse yet, he doesn't read at all). Some of the fine points are reviewed here. A full list of rules and conventions is offered at the end of this chapter. Round two of revision is a good time to check these issues.

- Every time a different character speaks, you should start a new paragraph. This is not only an important rule of dialogue, it is an attraction for your reader. A page that is filled with long paragraphs looks dense and uninviting.

Breaking up your paragraphs will have the opposite effect. It will invite your reader into your story.

- The end punctuation always goes inside the quotation marks. This includes periods, exclamation points, commas, and question marks. This is correct:

    "If I have to go to school, I'll run away," Emily said.

  or

    Emily said, "If I have to go to school, I'll run away!"

  or

    "Do I have to go to school?" Emily asked.

This is not:

    "If I have to go to school, I'll run away", Emily said.

  or

    Emily said, "If I have to go to school, I'll run away"!

  or

    "Do I have to go to school"? Emily asked.

- There is only one exception to the rule—and that is when a character or a narrator is repeating a passage of dialogue as a question or an exclamation, as in:

    Could it be that Emily meant what she said when she uttered, "If I have to go to school, I'll run away."?

Sentence Length and Variation

Subject-verb-object makes for a grammatically correct sentence, but it doesn't make for an especially interesting sentence. Varying sentence structure through the use of introductory and explanatory clauses, sentence fragments, and questions instead of statements can make your writing more interesting and lively.

Be careful, though. By attempting to make your writing more lively, you may make your sentences more complicated than they need to be. One way to avoid this trap is to analyze your story in terms of sentence length. Try to make your sentences around ten words in length. Keep in mind that this is an average number. Not all sentences need to be ten words or less. But if your story is full of sentences that are more than ten words—and averages fifteen plus—then you probably have a number of sentences that are too dense or more convoluted than they need to be.

Dated and Regional References

Another problem you will want to identify in round two revision is any reference that will sound dated or old-fashioned to children today. Unless your story is set in another era, your story's tone should sound contemporary. Because you are older than your audience, you may find these words and phrases difficult to weed out. Keep your audience in mind and how they may react to your story.

The same is true of regional references, regional slang, or phrases that will not be readily understood by your reader. The term soft drink is called different things depending on the part of the country. In the Midwest, it's called "pop." In the East, it's called "soda." And down South, any brand of soft drink is often simply just called a "coke." Choosing a common term rather than a regional one will ensure that your reader will understand what you are talking about. (In the example above, I would probably give up the notion of soft drink altogether and have my characters drink lemonade!)

CRITIQUES

After this phase of revision, you may want to seek the advice of others. You may be in a writers group that does regular critiquing. Or you may seek out the advice of a professional to review your work.

Many of these professionals advertise in writing magazines or in other publications. They often attend writers conventions to advertise their services. You may find some names in the phone book under *Writing Coach* or *Editorial Services*. Or you simply may know someone who is a children's writer or a writing teacher who is willing to look at your work.

Because children's books are a unique genre, it's best to find a professional who specializes specifically in juvenile literature. It's even better if you can find a specialist who has written in your genre.

Always ask for references if you are hiring a professional to review your work. Find out what kind of work she has done for other writers and whether the financial investment was worth it. Keep in mind that advice of this professional does not automatically mean you will be published. You are seeking one person's opinion. An editor at a publishing company may see your work in a completely different light.

If you choose to seek a critique, make sure that you know what kind of criticism you are looking for. Many writers are really just looking for affirmation rather than praise. If that's the case with you, skip the critique and show it to your mother or someone who will give you the praise you are seeking.

If you feel you need a critique, make a list of the specific issues you want feedback on. You should be looking for more than just whether it's good or bad. You're looking for weak spots you didn't know were there, for problems you overlooked because you were too close to the manuscript, and for concrete advice. If you feel your character development is weak, ask for specific opinions on that. If you are unsure of the marketplace for your work, ask about the marketplace specifically.

Just because you get that advice, you don't have to take it. If your work is being critiqued by a group of other writers just like you, writers who have not yet been published, their opinion is just as good as yours. And ultimately, it's not their opinion, but the editor's opinion that counts.

Be prepared to pay for the critique. You would not ask another professional for advice without remuneration, so don't expect it of the person who is doing your critique.

Finally, don't use the professional's name in a cover letter to a publisher as if it is an endorsement—unless your critiquer gives you permission to do so. Remember, they have a reputation in this marketplace. Don't compromise it for them.

Conferences often offer critique sessions, which can also be very helpful. Most of the time, the person in charge of the critiquing is either an editor or a published author. The critique usually involves a face-to-face meeting. This allows you to ask questions and clarify comments. It also gives you an opportunity to develop a relationship with a professional in the field.

ROUND THREE: THE MICROSCOPE

The final round of the revision process involves taking a very close look at every detail of the manuscript. If you have been doing your revision primarily on the computer, now's the time to print out your story, grab a pen, and really examine the hard copy of your work.

Your first step is to do a general read to check every element you examined before. Does the plot move along? Are the characters well-defined? Are the details of the setting integrated properly? You're probably tired of looking for these things, but you need to give the elements of the story one more once-over.

Spelling, Grammar, Punctuation, and Style

Your next step is to make sure every element of the manuscript is correct in terms of spelling, grammar, punctuation, and style. If you have a friend who is a whiz at these details or if you know someone who edits for a living, you may want to contact them to see if they can assist you in this final go-round. If you don't, you'll want to invest in one of the many good style guides to ensure that you know the rules of fine writing. These include *Words into Type* by Marjorie E. Skillin, et al, *The Chicago Manual of Style*, and the very readable *The Elements of Style* by William Strunk Jr. and E.B. White. You can find these tools at your library, but it's a good idea to purchase one or all of them so you have a reference readily available during the final stage of revision. (If you have them on your desk, you'll also be more likely to refer to them throughout the writing process.)

Don't rely exclusively on your computer's spell and grammar checks. Most spell checking programs don't catch synonyms or words that are used in the wrong context. And there are few adequate grammar and punctuation checking programs out there. Because your work is likely to be fiction, the programs will pick up phrases that are technically incorrect but are part of fiction's conventions. Sentence fragments, for instance, will always turn up on a grammar check, but those sentence fragments are likely to have been included for effect in fiction. Don't let your grammar checking program fool you into changing them.

Common Mistakes

You probably did not become a writer because you wanted to be an expert on grammar, punctuation, and style. The good news is you don't have to be. However,

COMMONLY CONFUSED WORDS

accept/except
already/all ready
by/bye/buy
its/it's
lie/lay
loose/lose
principle/principal
stationary/stationery
their/there/they're
through/threw
too/to/two
toe/tow
whose/who's
weak/week
weather/whether
which/that
whole/hole

there are a number of common mistakes writers make that cause editors to cringe. If you learn what these are, you'll be able to clean up your own writing.

Capitalization

It's a good idea to check every capital letter in your story to make sure that the word in question should actually be capitalized. The general rule is that if the word is a proper noun, it should be capitalized. One simple way to check a word is to simply use your dictionary. There are variations, though, and it's important to learn what they are.

When you use a term that can substitute for a proper name, like mom for instance, capitalize it only if a modifier does not precede it.

Correct:

I'll ask my mom if I can go.

I'll ask Mom if I can go.

Incorrect:

I'll ask my Mom if I can go.

I'll ask mom if I can go.

The other common capitalization mistake has to do with the names of places. Earth, when used in conjunction with the other planets, should be capitalized. When used independently, it should be lower cased. If you are referring to a specific region, it is correct to use capitalization.

Correct:

The South will rise again.

The southern states were in rebellion.

Mars is the closest planet to Earth.

You can find bodies of water almost anywhere on earth.

If you have a question about capitalization and you can't find the answer, use lower case. You'll probably be correct.

General Punctuation

As we discussed earlier, when using dialogue, the end punctuation of dialogue goes inside the quotation marks, whether that end punctuation is a period, question mark, or exclamation point.

Use exclamation points sparingly. And when you use them, use just one. Your reader will get the point. It's a good idea to look at every time you have used an exclamation point in your manuscript and really think about whether it is necessary.

Dot, Dot, Dot

Ellipses—those three periods that you often see in writing—are used for two reasons. They are used to show a pause in speech or they are used to show a trailing off in speech. If you are showing a pause—and you pick up the sentence after the pause—use three ellipses. If you are demonstrating a trailing off in speech, you also use three ellipses, but you add a period at the end to show that the sentence has ended. Again, use ellipses sparingly. Let the rhythm of your story allow for its own pauses, like these examples:

"The day seemed to last . . . well, forever."

"I don't think that I want to jump off . . . ."

Troublesome Commas

Commas are troublesome beasts, especially if you are using commas to punctuate a fairly long passage. Consult a good style guide if you have questions, but if you are unsure of where a comma goes, even after consulting your style guide, leave it out. The rule, "When in doubt, leave it out" works best here.

There are two ways, though, that you need to ensure that you are using commas correctly. The first is when you are describing a series of three things. You have the option of using a series comma—a comma before the last item mentioned—or leaving that comma out. Whatever you decide, you need to be consistent throughout your work. I prefer the series comma, but either of the sentences below is correct:

I asked for peanuts, hot fudge, and vanilla ice cream.

I asked for peanuts, hot fudge and vanilla ice cream.

The second place to double-check commas is in your dialogue. If you are using a tag line following your dialogue, you should place a comma inside the quotation mark. If you are using a tag line before a passage of dialogue, position it before your first quotation mark, as shown here:

"I can't wait until school starts," Phillip said.

Phillip said, "I can't wait until school starts."

Plurals and Apostrophes

Apostrophes indicate two things: possessives and contractions. They do not indicate that a noun is plural. This is a common mistake, but it's a serious one. At best, it looks careless. At worst, it looks amateurish. Look at every apostrophe in your story and make sure that it is used to indicate either possessives or contractions.

While you are at it, take a hard look at your contractions. Every time you use the word *its* or *it's*, make sure you have used it correctly. *Its* is a possessive form; *it's* is a contraction for "it is." Check the contraction *they're* and make sure you don't mean *their* or *there*. Take a look at *your* and *you're* as well. Make sure you weed out these rudimentary problems in the third round so that your manuscript looks professional.

Italics

Italics are used for emphasis and to indicate book titles or titles of other creative works.

Italics should also be used to indicate inner dialogue or a character's thoughts, but italics should only be used when you are in third person, not first person. In first person, the entirety of the story is really the main character's inner dialogue. There's no need to indicate this to the reader through the use of italics.

Quotation Marks

As a general rule, quotation marks should be used to indicate dialogue only. Chapters of books are also put in quotation marks, as are short stories, but it is unlikely that you will have included these in your story.

Avoid overusing quotation marks to indicate euphemisms. The use of quotation marks below is probably overdone, although it is not technically incorrect:

She was a classic "do-it-yourselfer."

He was a real "wolf in sheep's clothing."

Spellings

Use accepted, United States spellings rather than British or Canadian variations: *theater*, not *theatre*; and *gray*, not *grey*. When using a word that has variant spellings, choose the first choice in the dictionary and stick with it. If you decide to spell the word *T-shirt* with a capital *T*, don't change your spelling to *t-shirt* later in the manuscript.

HOW LONG SHOULD ALL THIS TAKE?

Revision takes various amounts of time, depending on how workable your first draft is and how often you return to your work. It will almost always take more time than you anticipated. And it will probably take at least three times as long as it took you to develop your very first workable draft. You may also find that shorter books—picture books, for example—take you longer to revise than longer, middle grade novels. That's because every word in a picture book really counts. With only thirty pages or so of real writing space, picture books need to be sharpened to an incredible degree.

Some writers find it helpful to work on several projects at once, revising at various intervals. Most writers, though, get caught up in a story and want to focus on just one piece at a time. Whatever you choose to do, know you are perfecting your craft. Revision is hard work, but it is essential work. In the end, a well-revised manuscript is a well-received manuscript, and it will get at least a first look from a publisher.

USE ITALICS FOR:

Book titles

Magazine titles

Play titles

Works of art

Television programs

Software programs

Names of ships, trains, aircraft

Inner dialogue, if the story is told in third person

THE MANUSCRIPT DOCTOR

One good way to ensure the next manuscript you write takes less revision time is to notice what kinds of revisions you are making through the three rounds. Then, you will know the pattern of your revisions—the kinds of problems you experience and the kinds of mistakes you make consistently—and can avoid them or weed them out easily. Use the worksheet below to help.

Round One Revision

1. Is your plot too complicated? (Are you able to sum up your plot in a couple of sentences?) How is it too complicated?

2. Where do you overwrite your story?

3. Where do you underwrite your story?

4. Does your story pass the "read aloud" test?

5. Does your story make sense?

6. Is your story responsible?

7. Do grown-ups impede the story's plot or message?

8. Does your story feel as if it is important enough to be a picture book?

9. Where are places where description slowed your story down?

Round Two Revision

1. What kind of problems do you encounter with your:

Opening

Body

Resolution

2. Do you use adequate transitions?

3. Do you stray from your main character's point of view?

4. Where do you tell instead of show? (Many editors and critiquers actually use the shorthand *SDT* to represent passages that show instead of tell.)

5. Do you use past tense throughout?

6. Where do you overuse passive voice?

7. Does your dialogue move the plot forward? Are there sufficient tag lines?

8. Do you vary your sentence length and structure? How many sentences are more than ten words in length or are convoluted in structure?

Round Three Revision

1. Where do you have to correct capitalization?

2. Is your end punctuation properly positioned?

3. How many times do you overuse ellipses?

4. Are you having comma trouble? How many times have you scrutinized or changed your commas?

5. Do you need to correct quotation marks?

6. Do you use accepted spellings?

DIALOGUE EXERCISE

Edit the passage below, removing both chitchat and stiff words and phrases.

"Hello, son," Mr. Smith said. "It's certainly a nice day today."

"Yes, indeed it is," Jeff responded. "I wasn't very sanguine about the weather, so I am glad it cleared up."

"I am too. However, I am worried that it might rain tonight," Mr. Smith said.

"Why would that be of concern?" Jeff questioned quizzically.

"It's our big chance to prove to Northville High that our baseball team is superior," Mr. Smith answered. "If it rains, the game might be cancelled."

Edit the passage below, using proper punctuation and changing the tag lines that do not represent speech.

"The joke we pulled on Mr. Mooney was a riot!" Jennifer laughed!

"I agree," Melanie snorted. "I've never seen anything so funny in my life."

"He looked absolutely hilarious, crazy and stupid, with that bucket on his head," Jennifer chortled.

All of a sudden, Melanie realized Mr. Mooney was standing right behind her!!!

"I didn't think this was at all funny." Mr. Mooney glared.

"I-I didn't really think it was funny," lied Melanie. "Jennifer is the one who is making me laugh about it."

Revise this passage of dialogue so it reflects the patterns of natural speech, including gestures, pauses, reactions, and descriptions. Keep the passage in Beth's point of view.

Beth and Julie walked slowly home. Beth saw a puppy up ahead of them. The puppy was limping, as if it were hurt.

"Hey, look at that puppy," Beth said.

"He looks like something is wrong with him," Julie said.

Beth asked, "Do you think we should help him?"

"We probably should, but my mom always tells me to stay away from stray dogs," Julie said.

Beth said, "I know, but he really looks hurt. What should we do?"

IT'S A DATE

See how many dated references you can find in the passage below. I've underlined one example:

> Mary sighed. She knew that she should call her grandmother. After all, today was her birthday. She watched as her mother picked up her <u>compact</u> and put it in her pocketbook. Her Shirley Temple curls were tied back with organza ribbon. She jumped off the davenport and headed to the phone. As soon as she picked it up, she knew she didn't want to dial it. It was always difficult talking to her grandmother. She repeated herself so much it was like listening to a broken record.

WRITING GROUP GRABBER

Choose several passages from the opening pages of classic works of literature. *The Giver, Charlotte's Web, Moby Dick,* and *The Adventures of Huckleberry Finn* are good choices. Revise these passages and then compare your revisions. Discuss why you think the authors did not make the revisions you have made.

7 MARKET RESEARCH

Getting your manuscript published requires a number of factors to converge at one time. Luck can play into it, but solid writing and an engaging story are of utmost importance. Following the rules for length, age group, and book category is essential. A polished manuscript impresses an editor. But one of the most critical tasks you will face in your search for publication is market research—knowing which publisher(s) to approach, and when and how to approach them.

If you have tried to research the marketplace for children's books, you've likely come away confused. There are literally hundreds of publishing companies, usually called publishing *houses*, in the United States and Canada, as well as abroad. Only a fraction of them publish children's books. And within that small percentage most publishers have their own niche and specialize in specific kinds of books.

CHILDREN'S BOOK PUBLISHING 101

To make the best decision about which publisher is best for your manuscript, you should learn as much about the business of children's publishing as possible. Learning about the business isn't difficult; it is, however, sometimes hard for children's writers, who write for all kinds of noble and admirable reasons, to believe that it is a business affected by the same economic conditions as other businesses. Though you may find it hard to believe, rejection is as much about the business of publishing as the quality of your manuscript.

There are several partners in this business. There are the publishers who are looking to publish books that create revenue for their stockholders and owners. The important word here is *revenue*. Revenue is profit, and books need to be produced profitably in order for the publisher to recoup what they invested. Generating raw sales isn't enough. Those sales have to be generated profitably; author's advances, any promotional and advertising expenses, the cost of printing the book, and the overhead of the publishing company have to be factored in before the publishing company makes one dime. The editor who is reviewing your story has to be absolutely sure that she can recoup any investment the company is making in publishing your book. It is not an easy decision.

The second partner in the business chain is the bookstore, mass-market outlet, or library distributor who purchases the book at a discount, usually around 50 to 55 percent off the suggested retail price. The bookstore outlet or distributor partners with the publisher to make sure that the book reaches the customers—the book buyers—at the end of the chain. They often cooperate in advertising, promotional campaigns, and sales efforts. Bookstores and distributors have their own revenue needs as well. Bookstores pay the booksellers in their stores. They also employ buyers, the individuals who make their book selections, their warehouse staff, and their marketing and support people.

The final partner in the support chain is the book buyer—the customer who visits a bookstore, goes to an online shopping outlet, or visits a mass-market outlet to purchase a book. This buyer may be a child or an adult. The general rule is the younger the book, the more likely it is to be selected by an adult. The buyer may be making this purchase for a number of reasons: She (the buyer for children's books is usually a female) may know an author's work, may be buying the book as a gift, or may be buying the book to encourage her child to become a better reader.

THE CHANGING BUSINESS

You may have preconceived notions of what the juvenile book publishing business is like based on your own childhood memories. Be prepared to give up those notions. In the past, children's book publishing was a small business. It generated income, but not significant revenue when compared to the rest of the publishing industry. Publishers brought out a number of new titles every year. These new titles are called the frontlist. Publishing companies relied on the classics they had already published—their backlist—to provide much of the revenue that supported the publishing and marketing process. Mainstream publishing companies publishing for adults relied on the blockbuster frontlist best-sellers. Such publishers had big budgets to promote their new authors as well; juvenile publishers relied on simple word of mouth, school visits, and small publicity tours to support their sales.

All of this has changed. Children's publishing today resembles adult publishing in many significant ways. Authors are getting more attention, more promotion, and larger and more elaborate book tours. Today, children's publishing companies rely more on their frontlist than their backlist. And, most importantly, children's publishing is looking for a blockbuster—just as the adult publishing field is.

THE ECONOMY MAKES THE WORLD GO 'ROUND

The most influential factor in the publishing business is the same as in any other business—the economy. Sluggish retail business means sluggish publishing. In tough economic times, publishers will publish fewer books and fewer risky books. To offset an economic downturn, they focus on publishing books from tried and true authors they think will be surefire hits. And they will publish in tried-and-true categories—books with holiday tie-ins, sentimental stories, and books that supplement educational initiatives.

There are other factors that affect the decisions of publishing companies. The price of paper may negatively impact the number of books a publisher can publish. An increase in paper prices in the late 1990s resulted in many books being postponed or cancelled.

Federal funding for public libraries, school libraries, and schools, all of which are major customers of children's books, also has a major impact on book purchases. When libraries and schools experience the pain of diminished budgets, publishing companies feel that pain.

Demographics, or population trends, also affect the profitability of publishing programs. When there are fewer kids in a particular age category, fewer books will be published in that category.

BOOK REVIEWS

As an editor is reading your manuscript, she is likely asking herself this question: Will this book review well? Book reviews in key trade magazines—*Publishers Weekly, School Library Journal, The Horn Book,* and *Booklist*—help bring the attention of books to book buyers at bookstores and library distributors. If a book receives a particularly positive review, a starred review in *School Library Journal,* for instance, the book purchase is almost automatic.

Just as important to the sales of the book are reviews in consumer magazines. Parenting magazines and women's magazines review books and make recommendations to parents. Large city newspapers also wield tremendous influence when it comes to reviews. The *Los Angeles Times, The New York Times, The Boston Globe,* and the *Chicago Tribune* are just some of the papers that can help spread the word about good books.

Another important factor in a buying decision—both by the consumer and the buyer at a bookstore or library—is whether or not the book has received an award. If the editor reading your manuscript thinks that it might qualify for a special award, she will be more compelled to give it a shot.

FACE OUT

Another factor an editor has to weigh as he is considering your manuscript is the merchandising practices of bookstores. Most bookstore chains have limited space to display children's books. Keep in mind the books selling in any given year aren't just new titles—they are backlist titles that remain on the bookstore shelves for at least a year if they are medium sellers, for three years or more if they are best-sellers.

If you've been to a children's section of a bookstore recently, you have probably noticed that there are a small number of books that are displayed face out, with the covers of their jackets showing. The children's section will likely feature a display of picture books, face out, and a number of point-of-purchase displays—spinner racks, tables with books, etc.—with the covers of the books showing. These displays may also offer shelf talkers, cardboard inserts that sit on the shelf below the book and point out the book's features. The bookstore may also feature end-caps, books displayed at the end of longer bookshelves. A rack of bargain books may be displayed next to shelves of other titles. Many of these bargain books may be displayed face out as well. Unlike other retail channels, where bargain merchandise is advertised, these bargain books are usually not called out in any way that the consumer might notice. They are simply lower priced than books that are written by well-known authors or published by well-known publishers.

What does this mean to the writer? Think about what it means to you as a consumer. What books do you see when you enter a children's book section? You probably notice the books on displays, end caps, tables, or bargain racks. If you are browsing or trying to decide to make a purchase on impulse, you have to pull books fairly randomly from the shelves, using the book spines only as your guide. If you know the author you are searching for, you should be able to find the book. And, of course, you will probably need to rely on the book department's bookseller to show you the way.

The bottom line for you as a writer and for the editor who is considering your manuscript: Bookstores make it very difficult for consumers to make impulsive purchases when it comes to kids' books. Getting your book published is only half the battle. Ensuring that it will get noticed is the real challenge. The editor who is reading your story has to be convinced that he can get your book noticed or he will probably decline to publish it altogether.

If you visit the children's section of bookstores often enough, you'll note that the displays are constantly changing. Bookstores take advantage of seasonality—especially of major and minor holidays—and publishers follow suit. In June, you'll no doubt note there is a seasonal table or display with frontlist and backlist titles displayed; often they're books or authors you may not have heard of before. Mother's Day, Valentine's Day, Martin Luther King Day, and Black History Month are also the impetus for new displays. (Christmas, Thanksgiving, and Halloween are obviously popular, too, but if you publish a book for these holidays, it may get lost in the crowd of other books.) The truth is this: If you can tie your book into a seasonal opportunity you'll have a better chance of getting maximum display time for your book—and that possibility will increase a publisher's interest.

NOT ALL BOOKS COME FROM AUTHORS

When you review a publisher's offerings, you may immediately think that every book on their list came from an author just like you, someone who submitted her manuscript to an editor. That is only partially true. Many American publishers acquire manuscripts from foreign publishers. American publishers purchase U.S. or North American rights to these titles, translate or Americanize them, and then bring them to market in the United States. Most of these foreign rights deals are completed at one of three overseas book fairs—the London Book Fair, the Frankfurt Book Fair, or the Bologna Children's Bookfair.

Of course, these books have authors, but the publisher does not deal with the author directly. Rather the sale is completed through the rights editors.

To show you the power of foreign rights sales, *Harry Potter and the Sorcerer's Stone* came to the U.S. in its American version because an editor at Scholastic discovered it at the Bologna Book Fair and was sure it would be a hit in the U.S. He negotiated the deal, and the rest, as they say, is history.

What does this mean to you as a writer? It means when you review a publisher's list or their catalog, only one half to three quarters of the books on the list were written by writers like you. While the publisher may publish one hundred books per year, for example, the company is really only looking for fifty to seventy-five original manuscripts from American-born authors. Your opportunities, then, have been slightly limited.

Some publishers buy more rights to foreign books than others. In general, the larger houses buy more rights than smaller ones. (These larger houses sell foreign rights as well.)

WHEN HARRY CAME TO TOWN

There is one important factor in recent times that has changed the economics of publishing—the Harry Potter phenomenon. The first Harry Potter book, *Harry Potter and the Sorcerer's Stone*, was an unprecedented best-seller, dominating the children's and the adult's best-seller lists. The sequels that followed also enjoyed best-selling success. The movies and video sales helped revitalize sales of the books in paperback.

What did this mean to the publishing industry? First of all, it increased the cool factor of reading. Kids who read Harry Potter were drawn to other books, and suddenly reading was a national habit, a habit that was admired. Secondly, Harry Potter drew people to bookstores in droves. (In the retail industry, this is called "increasing foot traffic.") Increased foot traffic meant increased sales—not just of Harry Potter books, but also of other books that were bought as add-on sales. Harry Potter also increased the legitimacy of children's literature. Since it appeared on both the adult best-seller list and the children's list, it became a valid book in both categories, paving the way for subsequent books to do big business in the same way. Finally, Harry Potter was offered not only in bookstores, but also in other retail outlets—warehouse clubs, discount stores, and even grocery stores. The end result? All kinds of books—in a wider variety than ever—are being offered at places other than traditional bookstores. No matter how you look at it, Harry Potter was good for the book business and for the children's book business especially.

The Harry Potter phenomenon was affirmed by another best-selling title, one which also has appeared on both the adult and juvenile best-selling lists. *Holes* by Louis Sachar, which was published in 1999 and won both the Newbery Medal and a National Book Award, experienced a resurgence in sales when the movie was released. Adults and children alike bought the paperback movie tie-in.

Another factor that is legitimizing children's books is that many writers who have only written for adults are now writing for juveniles. (Joyce Carol Oates and Toni Morrison are notable examples.) This may demonstrate a breakthrough in publishing in general. If adults are reading books created for children, juvenile books will no doubt continue to become more high profile, both in the attention they receive from the media and in the overall sales and revenue they generate.

READING FIRST

Another important phenomenon positively affecting the publishing industry is the renewed emphasis on reading in schools across the country. Federal legislation makes schools accountable for the success of their students in two key areas: reading and math. Federal funding is supporting the purchase of educational materials as well as trade books for classroom use. While states can use this money as they choose, many are directing funds toward purchases of classroom libraries—sets of picture books and other kinds of books for classroom use. While this has not quite caused the stir in the industry as Harry Potter has, it is still good for the publishing business.

BIG HOUSE/LITTLE HOUSE

Publishing houses, like all businesses, come in all sizes. There are five large houses that publish a full range of books for children of all ages and in all categories. They are Random House, Simon & Schuster, Scholastic, HarperCollins and Houghton Mifflin. These houses account for about half of the books (around four thousand to five thousand titles) sold each year. Smaller houses tend to specialize in market niches (Christian, educational, etc.) and publish fewer titles.

One of the most confusing publishing trends is the role of mergers and acquisitions. Large publishing houses are constantly taking over smaller houses. Publishing companies that were once independent are now owned by large houses. And, in turn, those large houses are owned by large conglomerates that have other interests and business ventures beyond publishing.

Golden Books, for example, a traditional children's picture-book line that published such classics as *The Poky Little Puppy*, one of the best-selling children's books of all time, was once independent. Random House now owns it. Dorling Kindersley Publishing, the innovative nonfiction publisher that changed the look of nonfiction throughout the industry, was once independent. It is now owned by the Penguin Group, which in turn, is owned by Pearson. An important lesson for writers is this: In a down economy, fewer acquisitions are taking place, which means information about publishers and who owns them is more consistent.

What does this mean to you as a writer struggling to get your manuscript read? It means the editor who had your manuscript on his desk last week may have left or been reassigned to another imprint. It also means that a company that appears to be a small publisher may actually be part of a larger conglomerate. If you were hoping to get extra attention from that small, cozy publishing house, you may find your hopes dashed if that small house has become part of a big corporation.

One other phenomenon that is important to note is the fact that bookstores are also becoming publishers. Barnes & Noble and Borders both publish their own books. They often buy foreign rights, but they also work with book development houses (explained on page 106) to create their books. They sell these books under their own imprints in their children's section. This limits the amount of shelf space available for books from other publishers and, in turn, limits the opportunities for children's writers.

IMPRINTS AND IDENTITIES

As you start doing your market research, you may find yourself confused by the difference between an imprint and a publishing house. Most publishing houses publish a variety of children's books under a variety of imprints. Each imprint has a different name and, usually, a distinct approach. Some imprints may be paperback only while others may publish hardcover and paperback. When imprints are particularly well defined, it's as if all the books in that imprint speak with once voice. This is not surprising since a single editor is usually responsible for contracting and controlling all of the titles in a single imprint. An imprint usually has its own editorial and marketing staff, but it shares most of the other functions with the larger publishing company of which it is a part.

To illustrate the difference between a publishing house and an imprint, consider Harcourt. Harcourt publishes a wide variety of materials for adults and children, including textbooks. Harcourt Children's Division publishes books for children. Within Harcourt Children's Division, there are these imprints: Gulliver Books, Silver Whistle, Voyager Books, Odyssey Classics, and Red Wagon Books. (While these imprints are clever references to stories or children's toys, other imprints are named for the editor who founded the imprint. At Scholastic, Arthur Levine, the editor who discovered Harry Potter, now has his own imprint called Arthur Levine Books.)

Often, a publishing company will develop a special imprint for serious literature and retain another for nonfiction or general interest titles. Millbrook Press, for instance, developed the imprint Roaring Brook Press for literary fiction, but retailed Millbrook for their nonfiction line.

Small publishing houses will generally have fewer imprints. They may, in fact, only have a single imprint—the publishing house's actual name. (Peachtree Publishers, Ltd., for instance, only publishes on the imprint Peachtree Publishers.) Large publishers generally publish a wide range of books for children, but they publish books in different imprints for different markets.

One way to investigate imprints is to page your way through a publisher's catalog. Most large publishers have a single catalog that features all of their imprints, each imprint in a separate section. This allows you to really hear the thematic voice of each imprint and get a sense of the kinds of books they publish. (To get a publisher's catalog, write a letter to the publisher and include a self-addressed stamped envelope.)

ALL KINDS OF BOOKS

You already know that there are different kinds of books aimed at different age children. You may not know that there are also different kinds of books aimed at different market channels.

Trade Books

Trade books are sold mostly through bookstore chains and small independent bookstores. In children's publishing, trade books are generally hardcover with book jackets and have features that deem them literary—such as rich and detailed artwork, lyrical story lines, or big-name authors. Novelty books, joke books, collections of ghost stories, etc., are usually not considered trade books. Trade books are generally priced over fifteen dollars.

The retail outlet for trade books is dominated by the two largest bookstore chains: Barnes & Noble and Borders (which also owns B. Dalton and Waldenbooks). Books-a-Million is a smaller bookstore chain, but is influential as well, especially in the South. When the economy is sluggish, these bookstores make smaller buys from publishers so publishers tend to publish fewer trade books. Most large publishers publish between forty and fifty trade books a year, in all categories.

In addition to the big chains, there are a wide variety of bookstores that are independently owned. These specialty stores tend to take a downturn or go completely out of business in a down economy. On the other hand, they thrive when the economy is thriving. They may offer children's books exclusively, or they may offer a range of all books and have a children's department.

Mass-Market Books

Mass-market books are generally sold through mass-market channels—discount stores, drug stores, supermarkets, and the like. They are targeted at a more general audience and are usually lower-priced. They are often offered in paperback rather than hardcover. In the mass-market arena, you will likely find joke and novelty books, as well as series titles, movie-tie-ins, etc. This particular channel of sales thrives in a down economy. Most larger publishers publish many more mass-market books than trade books—sometimes as many as five hundred a year. The average price for a mass-market book ranges from $1.99 (for a coloring book) to $10.00 (for a picture book).

Library Books

Books that are sold to institutions, such as libraries, schools, and school libraries, tend to be nonfiction or educational, hardcover, and to use special binding for durability. Trade books are also sold to the institutional market. Federal and state level funding for libraries and schools impacts the institutional market. When funding dries up, so do book purchases. In addition, the emphasis on technology in the school and library environment has meant that these institutions have diverted funds from buying books to buying computers, software, and special Web-based programs.

Smaller publishers generally specialize in a single kind of book and in selling through a single market channel. Lerner Publishing Group, for example, sells primarily to the school library and public library market.

While these categories hold generally true for the marketplace, there is, of course, much crossover. High-quality literary titles are sold in mass-market chains, mass-market books are sold in bookstores, and so on. There are also specialty Christian bookstores, toy stores, museum shops, and other outlets that sell appropriate books to their customers.

Why Does All This Matter?

You may not know whether your manuscript fits the trade, mass-market, or institutional category. And you may not know whether it is right for a particular publisher or a particular imprint. Furthermore, you may not really care. You've written a story; you just want to see it in print. But knowing that publishing is a business—and how that business works—makes you an insider. And that's an important advantage in making decisions about your particular piece of work.

READY, SET, RESEARCH!

There are many resources at your fingertips that will help you learn who is publishing what and whether they currently accept unsolicited manuscripts.

Market Guides

Market Guides list what a particular publisher's needs are. They are generally updated with new information every year. The best of these, *Children's Writer's & Illustrators Market*, published by Writer's Digest Books, lists both book and magazine publishers, offers market hints, features real life success stories, and other information. There are several other guides as well, including the *Children's Writer's Guide* that can be ordered through the Institute of Children's Literature and the *Christian Writer's Market Guide*. The Society of Children's Book Writers and Illustrators also publishes its own guides electronically and on paper—for a reasonable price if you are a member. Their guides cover the children's book market, as well as the children's magazine market. (For more information on The Society for Children's Book Writers and Illustrators, see page 107.)

There is one problem with relying entirely on market guides. As soon as they are in print, no matter how often they are updated, they are out of date. That's why it's important to rely on several sources of information when doing your research. In the competitive world of publishing, publishers change strategy all the time. Other publishers or conglomerates also buy publishers. And, unfortunately, some simply go out of business.

Industry Guides

The Literary Marketplace is the guide to the publishing industry. *The Literary Marketplace* is helpful to beginning writers because it is a comprehensive guide to all of the services a writer or publisher could ever need. It not only features publishers, it offers information about printers, publishers, agents, freelance editors, and book development houses.

Book development houses, sometimes called packagers, are businesses that develop manuscripts, often from start to finish. They hire the writers, illustrators, and designers necessary to create a book and then sell their services to publishers. Book development houses often provide detailed outlines to the writers that they hire. They generally pay a flat fee and sometimes require that the author act as a ghostwriter for the creator of a book series.

Book development houses are a great way for prepublished authors to get a start. They are always looking for new talent and for writers who can write to formula. Development houses often let writers "try out" for particular series, purely on speculation. They may offer to send a writer an outline, some character sketches, and some overall ideas, and evaluate his suitability for freelance writing opportunities.

Writer's Guidelines

Most writers don't realize that publishers make it fairly easy for writers to research the market. Most publishers offer their own guidelines that detail what they publish, how they want manuscripts submitted, and whether they are accepting unsolicited manuscripts. The guidelines will also tell you what they don't publish. Some publishers don't publish in specific genres. If your manuscript is in that genre, there is no point in sending it—no matter how good it is. To get guidelines, you simply need to send the publisher a self-addressed stamped envelope or visit their Web site.

Publishers' Catalogs

Publishers also provide catalogs of all their frontlist titles, titles that they are publishing in the coming six months, as well as a listing of their backlist titles, titles that they published in previous years. Studying these catalogs closely can give you some important insights into what that publisher is publishing and what themes and topics they are looking for.

When you are analyzing publishers' catalogs, consider how much of their frontlist appears to be fiction? How much is nonfiction? Does it include other kinds of books—like craft books, activity books, etc.? Break the frontlist and backlist down by a general percentage, and you'll be able to determine how many books this publisher *really* publishes in each category. (This information may either support or contradict what you've found in publishers' guidelines.)

Does the catalog offer information on promotional and advertising campaigns? Do they offer information on print runs? You can determine what kind of book the publisher really puts its money behind by checking out this information, which is generally printed along with the book blurb. If the publisher is putting a great deal of backing behind several young adult titles, for instance, you'll know that young adult books get extraordinary attention at that particular house.

Does the catalog offer information that sounds as if it is geared toward teachers or librarians? Does it offer grade levels instead of age levels or reading levels, or does it refer to established reading programs, such as accelerated reader? If you find these references, you can be sure that the publisher sees schools and libraries as a large part of their market. They are a good candidate for nonfiction, early readers, or the institutional books mentioned earlier.

Organizations, Newsletters, and Conferences

As I mentioned earlier, a good source of information about publishers is the Society of Children's Book Writers and Illustrators (www.scbwi.org). In addition to their market guide, they publish a bimonthly newsletter that offers the latest news about who is publishing what. They also sponsor international and regional conferences that feature editors and authors who can give you insider information about what publishers are publishing. Often, conferences allow the opportunity for a face-to-face critique of your manuscript by an editor. Through this critique, you can establish a relationship with an editor that may help get your manuscript more personal attention.

Other helpful organizations include the Children's Book Council (www.cbcbook s.org), a professional organization to which most publishing companies belong. While they primarily serve publishing companies, the information they provide is valuable to writers as well.

In the book selling arena, there is one major organization—the American Booksellers Association—that brings publishers and booksellers together. This organization has one annual meeting a year, called BookExpo America that draws from the entire country. Among other things, the expo features a large trade show during which publishers unveil their latest titles. While the national show can be overwhelming, smaller regional meetings are held throughout the country as well, and these meetings offer a terrific opportunity to see firsthand what is being published.

The International Reading Association, The American Library Association, and the National Council of Teachers of English offer both regional and national meetings. These organizations are primarily for professional teachers and librarians, but attending a meeting—even a regional meeting—can offer you insight into the marketplace.

Trade Magazines

Publications like *Publishers Weekly* and *School Library Journal* provide both book reviews and news stories about what publishers are publishing. Twice a year, in the spring and fall, *Publishers Weekly* publishes a children's books announcement issue that introduces forthcoming titles. *Publishers Weekly* also provides an industry news section that can tell you who has been promoted, and who has changed positions or publishing houses.

Bookstore/Library Research

Visiting a bookstore or library is another good way to discover who is publishing what, but you have to be careful to train your eye to identify books by their *publishers*, not by their theme, story, or author.

It's also valuable to make notes on how your local bookstore merchandises their books. Which books are showing face out? Which are displayed on tables? How often does the merchandising program change? In short, what books seem to be getting the most attention? This can help you determine how to effectively position your book with a publisher; if Barnes & Noble is giving attention to a certain kind of book at a certain time of year by placing it face out, you can make the case that your book might garner the same attention. (Consider your subject matter and determine whether it meets seasonal criteria, like back to school, or if it follows some other trend that is attracting children's attention.)

By the same token, it is valuable to check out mass-market and warehouse clubs looking for the same things. Their merchandising programs will be different from bookstores, as will their book mix. What differences do you notice? What similarities?

Web Research

There are many helpful Web sites that can provide you with information that will help you develop market savvy. You'll find them listed in the resources section. In addition to providing information, these sites often offer chat rooms where you can develop personal contacts that can help you further refine your research.

Newsletters for Children's Writers

There are several helpful newsletters for children's writers that offer market tips as well as writing support. *Children's Writer* offers monthly advice of trends in the publishing field and does a particularly good job of tracking the needs of children's periodicals. *Children's Book Insider*, also a monthly, offers information on technique and trends. *Once Upon A Time* is a quarterly magazine for those interested in children's literature and in writing and illustrating children's books. The Society for Children's Writers and Illustrators also provides a newsletter called the *Bulletin* to their national membership. This newsletter features a very valuable section called The Publisher's Corner that tells which publishers are acquiring and what they are looking for. Some regional chapters of SCBWI also publish their own newsletters, some of which contain information about market trends.

Personal Contacts

You can also rely on personal contacts—one of the "tools" mentioned earlier—to feed you information. These contacts may be librarians, teachers, bookstore clerks, publishing sales reps, or other authors. Of these, publisher's sales reps may offer you the most insider information regarding various publishers. To find out how to contact a publisher's representative, buddy up to a bookstore clerk. She can give you information and possibly provide a referral to a publisher's rep.

THE TERMS AND THE TRUTH

As you begin your research into various publishers, you will no doubt run into certain terms. It's important to know these terms because they are part of the rules of children's publishing.

One of the phrases that you will read when you begin your research is the term *unsolicited manuscript*. Many publishers will state that they do not accept unsolicited manuscripts or unsolicited submissions. An unsolicited manuscript is a manuscript an author sends to a publisher without the publisher's invitation or without the involvement of an agent. This is particularly disheartening news for writers who have found the perfect publisher for their book, yet discover the publisher is not accepting unsolicited manuscripts.

But take heart. Most publishers have flexible policies about unsolicited manuscripts; when they have filled their capacity for manuscripts, they will declare a moratorium on unsolicited works. In other words, at some points in time, they *will be* accepting unsolicited manuscripts.

Publishers also make exceptions to this rule. Some publishers that do not normally accept unsolicited manuscripts will do so for members of the Society of Children's Book Writers and Illustrators. If you've attended a conference and met an editor in person, that editor may be willing to consider your manuscript regardless of standard policy.

All in all, though, whether or not a publisher is accepting unsolicited manuscripts is determined by how badly they need to find books to publish. If the economy is robust and books are selling well, they will be more likely to dip into that slush pile of manuscripts. If the forecast for the economy is flat in the book business, they will tighten things up and rely on their tried-and-true authors or on economical rights deals with foreign publishers.

FIND YOUR GUIDE

Using a market guide, such as *Children's Writer's & Illustrator's Market*, or the Internet, find the children's imprints of these larger publishing houses.

Scholastic, Inc.

HarperCollins Publishers

Random House

Using the same market guide, identify three smaller publishers that publish less than twenty-five titles per year.

What is the predominant niche for these publishers? Here are some examples for you to consider:

Christian

Educational

Picture Books

Special Needs

Reference

Multicultural

Other

Visit the Web sites for the above publishers. Are writer's guidelines posted? If not, does the Web site indicate how to obtain them?

Using today's paper or another news source, identify three trends that may affect the publishing business. Use these categories as your guidelines:

Demographics, population trends:

Educational issues:

Economic/retail factors:

Review the sources of publishing information above. Rank them according to ease of personal access from 1-5. Number 1 means that this resource is readily available to you; Number 5 means that it will be extremely difficult to access that resource.

Writer's guides

Publisher's guidelines

Catalogs

Organizations, newsletters, conferences

Trade magazines

Bookstores

Personal contact

YOUR BEST PROSPECT

Review *Children's Writers & Illustrator's Market* and identify three publishers who are likely to publish what you've written. Then begin to compile information about that publisher using a worksheet similar to the one below. I've completed the first one for you using a made-up publisher as an example:

Publisher: Little Red Hen Books

Categories of publishing:

Picture books

Nonfiction books for younger readers (Kindergarten-grade 2)

Special features:

Does not publish books with Christian themes

Will not accept poetry

Looking for new authors for nonfiction series

Is publishing unsolicited manuscripts

Next, compare the information above to the writer's guidelines once you have received them. Do the guidelines contradict or add anything to the information you have compiled? If they do, add that to your checklist.

Categories of publishing:

Picture books

Nonfiction books for younger readers (Kindergarten-grade 2)

Guidelines indicate that Little Red Hen is now publishing nonfiction chapter books for beginning readers.

Special features:

Does not publish books with Christian themes

Will not accept poetry

Submission guidelines:

Looking for new authors for nonfiction series

Unsolicited manuscripts?   <u>Yes</u>   No

Now find two additional sources of information. This information might be *Publishers Weekly*, your local bookstores, information from SCBWI, a librarian or teacher, a newsletter, Web site, or the publishers' catalog. Use this to supplement the information above. Now your worksheet might look like this:

Categories of publishing:

Picture books

Nonfiction books for younger readers (Kindergarten–grade 2)

Guidelines indicate that Little Red Hen is now publishing nonfiction chapter books for beginning readers. Editor of chapter book series is Sally Jones. Looking for manuscripts for nonfiction chapter books that are high-interest and will attract boy readers.

Special features:

Does not publish books with Christian themes

Will not accept poetry

Submission guidelines:

Unsolicited manuscripts: <u>Yes</u>   No

Looking for new authors for nonfiction series

Authors should submit outline and one sample chapter, along with writing credits.

Once you have completed the worksheet, you really have two choices: (1) You can review the manuscript or manuscripts you have completed and see where they match up. Indicate that with a checkmark. Pursue the publishers who have the most significant number of "matches."

(2) Another direction you can take is to use what you have found about this publisher and write a story that reflects precisely what they are looking for. In this case, it sounds as if Little Red Hen Press has a strong need to publish a nonfiction chapter series—and the need is so strong that they are willing to consider outlines from authors. Here's an opportunity for you. If you can react in a timely manner,

with an outline that reflects a beginning nonfiction chapter book and features a high-interest topic, you may achieve publishing success in a way you didn't expect. And then you will have established the contacts you need at Little Red Hen Press to have more of your work considered.

YOUR BEST PROSPECT—A WRITER'S WORKSHEET

Publisher:

Categories of publishing:

Special features:

Submission guidelines:

Unsolicited manuscripts: Yes   No

CONFERENCE TIME

Identify three to five conferences that will take place in the coming year. Use the chart below to evaluate each one.

Conference:

Time:

Special offerings:

Speakers: How many of each will be attending and speaking?

Authors:

Literary agents:

Book editors:

Cost:

 WRITING GROUP GRABBER

Assign each member of your writing group a different publisher to research. Use the steps above as your research guide. Compile your information in a portable file with a carrying case. Update it as needed.

8 OFF TO THE PUBLISHER

Imagine this scenario:

An editor is sitting at her desk, surrounded by stacks and stacks of manuscripts. She reaches for one, a wicked smile on her face. The manuscript has smudges on it and does not contain a proper cover letter. She laughs a bloodcurdling laugh as she signs a rejection letter, muttering under her breath about what an idiot the writer is.

This scenario is an exaggerated version of how many writers see the manuscript submission process. Writers often view editors as poised to find any excuse to reject the manuscripts that they have tried so hard to produce. If the editor is in a bad mood or has a headache, many writers think their manuscripts will be rejected immediately. Too many times I've heard writers say, "I don't have a chance." It's simply not true.

THE TRUTH ABOUT SUBMITTING

As I emphasized in the previous chapter, publishing is a business just like any other business. Publishers are in the business of publishing books that sell; they aren't in the business of rejecting manuscripts. After all, if the editor in the above passage spent her editorial life rejecting manuscripts she wouldn't have her job very long.

While it may seem that catching the eyes and ears of an editor is an arbitrary process, nothing could be further from the truth. An editor's job is to publish good books that sell in the marketplace and provide the publishing company with revenue. Editors and the larger publishing houses of which they are a part wouldn't be in business if it weren't for authors. And, while there are a great many established authors writing children's books, the industry is always in need of fresh faces on the writing scene. Consider the fact that the Harry Potter author, J.K. Rowling, was once an unpublished, unknown writer, struggling to catch an editor's eye just as you are.

In truth, editors aren't in the business of rejection; they are in the business of finding the gem in those piles of unsolicited manuscripts on their desks. Believe it or not, they *want* to publish your work.

There are many activities, however, that pull editors away from doing the real work of editing and publishing. There are meetings with management, art and design, printers, and sales representatives. There are catalogs to prepare, profit and loss statements to puzzle over, and contract terms to negotiate. There are sales presentations, corporate training sessions, and editorial staffs to manage. All this means that editors have less time than they'd like to review the manuscripts on their desks. As a serious writer, you'll have better luck getting your manuscript read if you make it easy for them by following the conventional rules of manuscript submission.

MANY PUBLISHERS, MANY SUBMISSIONS

In the publishing business, it used to be standard practice for publishers to state that they did not accept multiple submissions (also called simultaneous submissions). A multiple submission is a manuscript that is sent to several publishers for consideration at once. Writers believed, probably erroneously, that sending a manuscript to a single publisher in an exclusive submission made that publisher react more positively. After all, the manuscript must be "hot stuff" if they are submitting it for a single publisher's eyes only.

Unfortunately, this is just not true. Publishing companies are against multiple submissions because it makes everyone's slush pile higher. If you are submitting your work to multiple publishers, and the members of your writing group are doing the same thing, many publishers are going to receive the manuscripts, and the multiple of all those manuscripts will soon be overwhelming. In some cases it is so overwhelming that publishers make the decision not to accept unsolicited manuscripts at all—and this is bad news for writers.

The best advice for writers: Be smart about where you submit your work. Every publisher in the *Children's Writers & Illustrator's Market* is not appropriate for your work. In actuality, your shortlist should probably have only three to five publishing companies on it. Start with those three to five and move outward from there.

Many publishers request that you inform the publisher that your work is a simultaneous submission. You can do this if you choose but there are few downsides for failing to inform the editor of this fact. Let's be realistic—you will probably accept the first offer you receive. And that means you'll simply need to withdraw your manuscript from the other publishers to which you have submitted it.

PUBLISHERS' PET PEEVES

1. Authors who expect a full evaluation of their unsolicited manuscript with suggestions for how to make their work publishable by that particular publisher.

2. Authors who expect an instant reaction from the publisher. They follow up by phone, fax, and e-mail the day after their manuscript arrives.

3. Authors who use the publishers' fax machine to submit their work.

4. Authors who call or query with an idea they want help developing or authors who want to talk through their plot on the phone before they send a manuscript.

5. Authors who submit their work to several publishers at once, but put the manuscript meant for one publisher in the package meant for another.

6. Authors who "invent" their own literary agencies so that they can fool the publisher into believing the work is agented. (It doesn't work.)

7. Authors who submit blindly and have no idea what the other titles on the publisher's list are.

8. Authors who submit multiple manuscripts at once in the same package to the same publisher.

9. Authors who submit crude illustrations with their work.

10. Authors whose manuscripts demonstrate that they do not understand the importance of respecting the children who are their audience.

THE AGENT DILEMMA

Good literary agents make it easier for editors at publishing houses to do their work. Literary agents know a particular editor's taste and will select manuscripts that match her tastes and needs. They often pair manuscripts with illustrators so the editor's job is halfway done by the time they review the manuscript package. And agents generally do a good job of weeding out manuscripts that aren't at all ready to submit to a publisher.

Literary agents also provide a valuable service to authors. They can get manuscripts directly into the hands of editors, while authors might not be able to accomplish that task themselves. They bring manuscripts from the bottom of the slush pile to the top. Once they sell a manuscript, they also negotiate favorable contract terms.

Agents may also give writers feedback on their writing, while many editors are too busy to do so. If an agent thinks your manuscript is worthy, but not quite ready for the market, he may provide revision suggestions. If the manuscript is rejected by a certain publisher, the agent will likely know why and be able to share that with you, the writer, while you may never ascertain that why from an editor.

How do you find an agent? It can be tough for prepublished authors. Most agents want to represent writers who have a track record of some kind. You'll need to go about researching an agent in the same way you researched publishers. There are several tools that can be helpful.

The Association of Authors Representatives (AAR) is a professional society of agents, all of whom are required to follow a strict list of ethical guidelines. One of the guidelines addresses the issue of reading fees. Agencies that are members of AAR do not charge writers a fee for considering their work. *The Literary Marketplace* offers a section that is devoted to agents, both domestic and international. *The Children's Writers & Illustrator's Market* features listings of agents and contact information, guidelines, and individual needs of each agency. The Society for Children's Book Writers and Illustrators offers a list of children's book agents free to members. And, just as writers conferences feature editors as speakers, they also frequently feature agents as well. Be sure to take advantage of any and all of those opportunities.

When you have narrowed down a list of potential agents, make sure that you do some additional research. Doublecheck to make sure that the agent is a member of AAR. Find out what books, especially children's books, this agent has placed. And be clear about the agent's expectation for compensation. (Most agents will take a 10 to 15 percent cut of your sales. Some will charge a reading fee. Make sure you know all of this up front.)

Finally, ask for a list of references and contact these references to determine whether the agent has treated her clients fairly.

While an agent can open many doors for you, don't make the mistake of thinking that getting an agent is a surefire way to get your book published. At the same time, don't use your inability to find an agent stop you from submitting your work. In children's publishing, unlike adult publishing, you don't always need an agent. The doors will crack open if you've done your homework and the business environment is conducive to the book you have written.

Introducing . . . My Book!

The first step in making it easy for an editor to get a sense of your story is to introduce your manuscript in a cover letter. Many writers agonize over their cover letters—to the point that they can't bring themselves to submit their work because their cover letter isn't right. Writing a cover letter isn't that difficult, so don't let the cover letter excuse stop you from taking the risk of submitting your work. A cover letter isn't a complicated piece of correspondence. It's not a billboard advertising your story or a lavishly written statement of why a publisher should publish your work. A cover letter is simply a letter that you include with your manuscript to introduce your story to the editor. Think of it as a handshake and introduction, and put aside the notion that a cover letter needs to have a gimmick or be written in flowery prose.

Keep in mind that the best handshake and introduction is short and to the point. It is also straightforward and provides the information the person needs to know to size up the story's potential. It may be helpful to know that an editor typically quickly scans the cover letter first to determine if the manuscript is even close to fitting his needs and if the author has any credentials. Then he turns to the manuscript. If the manuscript intrigues him, he returns to the cover letter and reads it in more detail.

Here are the basic components of a cover letter:

Paragraph 1: Tell the editor your book's title, its intended age group, and its category.

Paragraph 2: Tell the editor succinctly—in one or two sentences—what the plot of your story is. If you have done market research (which you should have), tell the editor why you think the story fits their particular philosophy or imprint.

Paragraph 3: Tell the editor about yourself if you have relevant information. If you are prepublished but have special knowledge about the topic, tell the editor what that special knowledge is. If you have published anything at all—even in local newspapers—make passing reference to that.

Paragraph 4: Thank the editor for taking the time to read the story and ask for its return in a self-addressed stamped envelope (SASE) that you have included. (This is optional. You can ask the editor to destroy the manuscript if they do not want to publish it. I recommend against this, however. The manuscript will seem to have more value if you ask for its return.)

As you write your cover letter, keep in mind, once again, that publishing is a business. Your cover letter is a business letter that, hopefully, will lead to the business transaction of publishing your work. At the bottom of the cover letter, indicate any enclosures you are sending with the manuscript.

THE MANUSCRIPT

The manuscript itself should be typed and double-spaced with adequate margins on either side. (Never submit a handwritten manuscript. These hit the rejection pile immediately.) The title of the manuscript should be typed about halfway down the page. Your name and address should appear in the upper left hand corner. An indication of the manuscript's length should be typed on the right-hand side at the top of the page.

If you are submitting a picture book and want to indicate where you feel the pages should break, add an extra half space between intended page breaks. (There is no need to indicate that page one could feature the title page, page two, the copyright page, etc.) Remember that ultimately this is the editor's choice to make. On the other hand you will look as if you have really thought about the story if you indicate page breaks. (As mentioned earlier, there is usually no need to submit a dummy with the manuscript.)

Use a standard typeface and use that typeface consistently throughout the entire manuscript. Don't use fancy fonts or vary fonts throughout. Print your manuscript on good, white paper stock, not flimsy computer paper. This is a business transaction, remember? Be professional and businesslike in your presentation.

There is no need to bind your manuscript in a fancy binder or even to staple it. If your manuscript is long, use a simple rubber band to hold the pages together.

How to Send It

The U.S. mail is still the choice of most publishers, but some publishers are now accepting manuscripts through e-mail. Check the publisher's guidelines and, if they do not specifically mention electronic submission, send it through regular mail. Never fax manuscripts to publishers; publishers use their fax for the daily business of the publishing house.

SAMPLE MANUSCRIPT FORM

Huckleberry Finn

Mark Twain Way

Rivertown, Mississippi

Social security or date of birth (optional) Approximately 500 words

THE DAY I MET TOM

By Huckleberry Finn

This is an example of correct manuscript form for a fiction or nonfiction book. Your name and address should be at the top of the page. The approximate length of your manuscript should appear in the right-hand corner. Then skip to about the middle of your page (sixteen to eighteen lines or so) and type your title in all caps. Type your name underneath your title. Then skip three or four spaces and start your story.

Use one side of the paper only and double space. Make sure that the margins are about 1.5 inches wide. You don't need to include a page number on page one of your story; begin numbering on the second page with page two.

QUERY LETTERS

You may have heard the term *query letter* either associated with magazine publishers or with some nonfiction submissions. As you read publisher's guidelines, you may find they suggest you query the publisher before you submit your work. A query letter can also be used if the publisher states that they are not accepting unsolicited manuscripts.

A query letter is much like a cover letter, but it is sent in advance of sending the manuscript itself. Because the query letter is not sent with the manuscript, its tone needs to be more sales-oriented. Your goal, in a query letter, is to entice the editor to ask to see the manuscript, and your message needs to be crafted to ensure that they do just that.

Don't send a query letter if the publisher states they are looking for complete manuscripts. If you do so, you've given up the chance to show off your story. All you are demonstrating is that you can write a query letter. You've also irritated the editor because you haven't followed the publisher's guidelines. It's always better to send a full manuscript if you are given that option. Still, if a publisher's guidelines require that you query first in their guidelines, you should follow their instructions.

How to Send It

Publishers are often very amenable to accepting queries over e-mail. Again, make sure you have read their guidelines carefully and they have indicated they are accepting electronic queries; if not, send your query through the U.S. mail.

PROPOSALS

Publishers will occasionally request proposals instead of a manuscript, especially for nonfiction work or for longer novels. A proposal generally contains a cover letter, a biography (of you, the author), a chapter-by-chapter outline, the first three chapters, and a book synopsis. You can really impress an editor if you also include a competitive analysis. What other books have been published on this topic? How is your approach unique and better?

How to Send It

Proposals are almost always sent through regular mail but electronic submission is an option if the publisher indicates this in their guidelines.

A WRITER'S WORRIES

When most writers get to this stage of the publishing process, they begin to worry and fret. In fact, some writers worry and fret so much, they never submit the manuscript at all. Here are some of the most common worries of writers at the submissions stage and how to overcome them:

I can't get my cover letter perfect. Do your best. If you really feel that you cannot write a cover letter that adequately introduces your story, send the manuscript without the cover letter, but send the manuscript.

The publisher will steal my story. Publishers simply don't steal stories. Besides, there are really no new stories under the sun. Your idea, in some form or another, has probably been proposed and published before. And, finally, you should know that you own the copyright to your story. Even if you haven't officially copyrighted the story, it is protected by copyright laws. In fact, officially registering the copyright is a waste of time and money. And including a copyright symbol on the manuscript itself makes you look naive and amateurish. By the act of writing the work, you own the work. Editors know this and as part of the publishing community, you should, too.

I've revised my story a thousand times, but I still don't think it's ready. At some point, you have to trust your story and yourself enough to take the next step and submit it. You can only rely on your writers group and your revision process so many times. The truth is, you won't get your story published unless you submit it. Take the risk. It may be worth it.

I've found ten publishers who are potential publishers for my work. Can I send it to all ten? Most publishers like to be informed if the work is a multiple submission. Other publishers don't accept multiple submissions at all. The guidelines will generally indicate their preferences. Remember, though, in the case of multiples submissions, consider a publisher's preferences simply that—preferences. There is very little downside to submitting your manuscripts to several publishers at once and *not* informing them. If one publisher accepts your work, simply write a note to the other withdrawing your manuscript.

You can make the process of submission more manageable, though, if you choose a small pool of publishers—say three to five—and submit to them first. After six months or when you hear back from them—whichever comes first—choose three to five more publishers and submit to them.

I haven't heard anything from the publisher. They must not have received my manuscript! The last thing you need to do in this situation is to make a hysterical call to the publisher to determine whether or not your manuscript was received. What you might want to do to avoid this situation is to include a self-addressed card in your manuscript package. Whoever opens the package will, presumably, return the card to you indicating that the publisher received it. It's not a fail-safe method; many publishers don't return the cards in a timely manner or at all, but when they do, it can provide peace of mind.

THE WAITING GAME

Waiting for a publisher to respond is one of the most tedious and self-defeating parts of the writing process. Most publishers take three months or more to respond to your manuscript. In the meantime, the writer who is waiting feels as if she is waiting for some kind of "final judgment."

The best thing you can do during the waiting game is to forget that you've even submitted the work. Mark the date on your calendar that is three months from the time you have sent your manuscript and get back to the business of writing. Occupy your mind with new characters, plots, and settings. Try a new genre or form. And, most importantly, submit something else. The more manuscripts you submit, the better the chances that one of them will be accepted. There is a law of averages at work, after all, that balances out artistic temperaments and business trends.

Three months is the average waiting time, but publishers may indicate that their own response time is longer or shorter. (You can find information about standard waiting times in *Children's Writer's & Illustrator's Market* as well as in publisher's guidelines.) After the prescribed waiting time, you can politely and professionally inquire about your manuscript. This is not the time to make demands, act impatient, or show your irritation, although all of these feelings are natural. Write a polite and businesslike letter requesting the status of the manuscript.

You may decide, at this point, to send the same manuscript to several different publishers. If you have informed the initial publisher that your work is an exclusive submission, that you are submitting it only to them, then you need to inform them you are circulating the work to other publishers. Again, do this in a professional and straightforward letter. No threats or accusations. They are in business—you are in business. If they can't accept your business transaction at this point, it's time to seek someone who might be able to.

THE THREE DEGREES OF REJECTION

There are three types of rejection letters: okay rejections, good rejections, and great rejections. The okay rejections are form letters that don't even address the author directly. These letters usually say something like, "Your manuscript does not meet our needs at this particular time." And that's usually what they mean. For whatever reason, the publisher cannot invest money in your manuscript. It's that simple. It doesn't mean the manuscript isn't good. It doesn't mean you aren't a worthy writer. It simply means they aren't able to make the business transaction needed to support your story.

You may get a form letter from a publisher with an encouraging, sometimes handwritten note, from an editor. This is a good rejection letter. It means that the editor has recognized your talent but, at the same time, cannot take the risk required on this particular manuscript. After you have finished patting yourself on the back, do the polite thing. Write the editor a note thanking him for his input and promising another submission soon. Don't wait to write the letter until you have a second submission ready. The editor has just paid you a compliment—you should respond immediately. Then get that submission together as soon as possible. Keep your name in front of that editor's eyes at all costs.

The best rejection letter is the one that offers a little constructive criticism about your story and suggests, if you are willing to revise it, the publisher might be interested in taking another look. Pat yourself on the back twice here. Then, once again, send the editor a quick note thanking him for his input and his time. Get to work on revision, as quickly as you can. Don't ask for additional input from the editor. He has offered you some feedback and given up as much time as he can spare. Also, don't imagine your manuscript will have a guaranteed sale because the editor has indicated interest. Things may change by the time you get the manuscript in the mail. At the same time the revision may not be quite what the editor had in mind and you may get a straight-out rejection.

THE BEST ANSWER—AN ACCEPTANCE!

If an editor has decided to publish your work, you will most likely hear over the telephone or via e-mail. The first call may be a bit vague in terms of the editor's intentions. The editor will no doubt tell you she likes the manuscript, she sees it as a part of one of her upcoming lists, and she may need a few revisions before she can fully commit to the project. She may also mention she likes the work, but she needs to run a profit and loss statement on the proposition or she needs to present it to her sales force. All of this is good news. It's highly likely that the publisher will publish your book, but you don't yet have a contract in hand. You haven't yet received a commitment.

If you receive a vague call like this, make sure that you set a time line with the editor. When will you hear back from her about a contract? Is there any information that she needs to help her sales team or her marketing team make a decision? (Here's where you can really shine. If you are willing to promote your book through school visits or bookstore signings, mention it now, even if you have already made a point of mentioning it in your cover letter.)

The reason the editor may be vague in the first phone call is because the nature of the retail business—of which book publishing is a part—can rapidly change. She wants to make sure her company is willing to take the financial risk of publishing your book and that the sales and marketing staff are willing to promote the book through advertising and face-to-face meetings with bookstores. The more enthusiastic they are, the more enthusiastic she will be, and the quicker she will be able to make a decision about a contract and terms.

She will probably discuss the nitty-gritty details in a second phone call. She will likely have a sense, by this time, of what kind of royalty she can offer you and what kind of advance against royalties she can afford to pay. A royalty is a percentage of every book sale, and it generally ranges from 4 to 8 percent of net proceeds. Net proceeds are defined as the amount of money a publisher receives from a book, after a standard bookstore discount of 55 percent off. Less frequently, the royalty is paid off list price. An advance is an upfront amount that a publisher will pay you, and you will eventually pay back in royalties. The advance is usually equal to the amount of money the publisher will earn on the printing of the first book. You won't start receiving biyearly checks until you have "earned back" the advance that was originally paid to you.

Most publishers will negotiate royalty amounts 1 to 2 percent. They may also offer escalation clauses—if the book sells a certain number of copies, you receive a higher royalty rate. After fifteen thousand copies are sold, for instance, you may receive 6 percent instead of 4 percent.

The advance is also negotiable. The advance is traditionally meant to pay for an author's time for the initial writing of the book. If you have already completed the manuscript and aren't required to revise it substantially, you may settle for a lower advance and negotiate for a higher royalty. (Advances range from three thousand dollars for a prepublished author to upwards of ten thousand dollars for a writer of reputation. Advances are much higher in adult books than they are in children's.)

Besides the royalty and advance, you will also have the opportunity to negotiate what are called subsidiary rights. Subsidiary rights are the rights and profits received when a publisher sells movie, television, or even merchandise rights like T-shirt rights. Generally, these rights are controlled by the publisher but profits are split 50/50 between the publisher and the author. Unless you have a friend in Hollywood who is dying to turn your book into a movie, it's best to allow your publisher to exploit these rights. If they land a movie deal, it is likely to be substantial money.

Other subsidiary rights include translation rights if a publisher sells your book internationally in a translated version. The proceeds from these rights are generally a few thousand dollars here or there, and you split them 50/50 with the publisher. Again, you should allow a publisher to control these rights unless you have specific contacts or you are working with an agent who can sell these rights for you in the international marketplace.

There are two negotiating points that you do need to fight for:

1. The copyright should be registered in your name.
2. The rights should revert back to you should the publishing company become insolvent or should they decline to keep the work in print after a certain period of time (three years is standard).

These two points are essential to your right to control your work. You wrote the work; you should hold the copyright. You will also have an easier time marketing the work to another publisher should your publisher decide not to keep it in print if you retain the copyright.

A rights reversion clause functions the same way. If the publisher does not keep the work in print for any reason, you have the right to take it to another publisher.

MAKING A LIVING

Once you've sold your first book, you may feel as if you are on easy street. Keep in mind that your advance, as far as advances go in the world of publishing, will be small. Remember, too, that it may be months before you receive a royalty check because you have to earn that advance back first.

In order to make a living in children's books, most authors look for revenue-producing opportunities that also allow them to promote and sell their work. One of the most rewarding is a school visit. During a school visit, an author visits a classroom as a kind of celebrity. He usually speaks about the process of writing his book in a large assembly or in individual classrooms. Writers who can provide hands-on writing activities are in particular demand.

If you want to pursue school visits, you should be comfortable with children and be able to organize a real program surrounding your book. You should also make contact with any organizations in your area that promote authors in schools. Your local SCBWI chapter is a good place to start. There are also literary and "artists in schools" organizations (usually run by a state or a community arts association) that already have established programs that you may be able to tap into.

Beyond school visits, consider visits to libraries, bookstores, and special events like book fairs in your community or surrounding areas. These events may not offer an honorarium, but they will offer you the opportunity to sell books, something your publisher will appreciate.

Very few children's book writers make their living simply by writing children's books. Recognize this, negotiate the best contract that you can, and then look for other opportunities, both paid and unpaid, to promote your work. You'll sell more books, make important contacts, and learn more about the children who are your audience.

Your Writing Workout

COVERING HANSEL AND GRETEL

Here is an example of a cover letter for the classic fairy tale Hansel and Gretel.

Tracey E. Dils
7777 Cherry Lane
Drury, Alaska XXXXX

Date

Jo March
Little Red Hen Press
89 Yellow Brick Road
Scarecrow, Kansas XXXXX

Dear Ms. March,

I am pleased to enclose *The Tale of Hansel and Gretel,* a picture book, for your consideration. This provocative book will delight readers ages three to seven, especially those who enjoy tales of enchantment and fantasy.

In *The Tale of Hansel and Gretel,* curious twins come upon a house completely constructed of candy in the woods. The two get more than they bargained for when they discover that the house belongs to a witch! Relying on their own intuition, the two eventually escape from the witch's clutches but not without learning an important lesson about following directions. The enchanting fairy tale-like quality and the child-centered plot make the book a perfect fit with Little Red Hen's Childstory picture book imprint.

I am a third grade teacher at Drury Elementary and have witnessed the power of fantasy literature firsthand in my classroom. I have written several nonfiction articles about various reading methods, and I have spoken at my local library about the role of literature in children's lives.

I have enclosed an SASE for the return of my manuscript should it not fit your needs. Thank you for considering *The Tale of Hansel and Gretel.*

Sincerely,
Tracey E. Dils
Enclosures: *The Tale of Hansel and Gretel.*

Using the letter on page 125 as a guide, write cover letters to accompany the following classic children's stories.

Little Red Riding Hood   *The Pied Piper of Hamlin*

Paul Bunyan   *Little Women*

Cinderella   *The Adventures of Tom Sawyer*

The Little Engine That Could   *Alice's Adventures in Wonderland*

The Three Little Pigs

TONE DOWN THE TENTATIVE!

The tone of your cover letter should by positive and strong. *I think* or *I feel* are weak phrases, and indicate a lack of confidence in your work. If you are submitting your work, you should feel strongly about its quality and its potential fit with the publisher.

Rewrite the following cover letter to remove tentative phrases.

Tracey E. Dils
7777 Cherry Lane
Drury, Alaska XXXXX

Date

Jo March
Little Red Hen Press
89 Yellow Brick Road
Scarecrow, Kansas XXXXX

Dear Ms. March,

I am pleased to enclose *The Mystery of Mallard Marsh*, a chapter book for early readers, for your consideration. I think the book will delight seven- to ten-year-old readers, especially those who are interested in nature and mysteries.

In *The Mystery of Mallard Marsh,* a young sleuth discovers a secret about how the mallards migrate through her town every year. I believe that its ecological theme, as well as its child-centered plot line, will make it a perfect fit for Little Red Hen Press's Young Mysteries chapter books series.

I feel my experience as a second grade teacher in my hometown of Drury and my experiences as a bird-watcher make me uniquely qualified to write about this subject matter. I think my additional writing experience—as a columnist for our local birdwatchng newsletter—is also proof of my writing skill. I speak to children on the topics of ducks and mallards at our local nature preserve and, I believe, this, too, is an important credential.

I have enclosed an SASE for the return of my manuscript should you choose to reject it. Thank you for considering *The Mystery of Mallard Marsh*.

Sincerely,
Tracey E. Dils
Enclosures: *The Mystery of Mallard Marsh*

DESCRIBE YOUR STORY

Make a list of adjectives that describe your story. Use a thesaurus to come up with additional descriptions. Here are some suggestions to get you started:

Compelling

Insightful

Unique

Distinctive

Lyrical

FIND THE ESSENCE

Review a manuscript you feel is ready to submit. Complete this passage by distilling the essence of the manuscript in two to three sentences. Refer to character, plot, and setting in as succinct language as possible. Use the most powerful adjectives from the above list that you can.

My story, _____, is about

SAMPLE QUERY LETTER

Tracey E. Dils
7777 Cherry Lane
Drury, Alaska XXXXX

Date

Emily Lawrence
Little Red Hen Press
89 Yellow Brick Road
Scarecrow, Kansas XXXXX

Dear Ms. Lawrence,

Have you ever imagined yourself lost in the woods? What if you were lost and came upon a house entirely made of candy? Children, ages three to seven, will delight in *The Tale of Hansel and Gretel,* a story of twins who discover that being lost in the woods is not a picnic.

In this enchanting story, told in lilting and lyrical language, Hansel and Gretel have to *rely* on their own intuition when they are captured by an evil witch who lives in a candy house! The enchanting fairy tale-like quality and the child-centered plot make the book a perfect fit with Little Red Hen's Childstory picture book imprint.

I am a third grade teacher at Drury Elementary and have witnessed the power of fantasy literature firsthand in my classroom. I have written several nonfiction articles about various reading methods, and I have spoken at my local library about the role of literature in children's lives.

Please let me know if you would like to read more about these two brave siblings. I enclosed an SASE for your response. Thank you for considering *The Tale of Hansel and Gretel.*

Sincerely,
Tracey E. Dils

127

QUERY LETTER

The cover letter shown for *The Tale of Hansel and Gretel* could be written as a query letter as shown on page 127. Using the rewritten version as your guide, rewrite the cover letters you have written for the fairy tales as query letters.

SYNOPSIS

A synopsis for Hansel and Gretel appears below. Using this as your guide, write a synopsis of the fairy tales previously listed.

Synopsis: Hansel and Gretel

In this delightful fairy tale, Hansel and Gretel venture into the woods behind their house, even though their mother has forbidden it. Deep in the woods, they discover a house made completely of candy. When they investigate further, they discover that the house is occupied by a witch. The evil witch holds the two captive, intending to eat her two victims. Relying on their own ingenuity, the two outsmart the witch and escape from her lair. They return safely home, having learned a valuable lesson about following the rules.

WRITING GROUP GRABBER

Have members of your writing group exchange manuscripts with each other. Then have each member write a query or cover letter based on the manuscript they received.

9 SOME SIMPLE INSPIRATION

As you've learned, there is no magic formula for writing and publishing children's books. This book has asked you to develop a road map, to work on craft, to hone your skill through exercises and worksheets. But there are two simple things you can do to become a children's writer:

Write as much as you can.

Submit as often as you can.

Let's take each of the ingredients of this secret formula separately.

What does it mean to write as much as you can? It means that you take every opportunity to write something, even if it isn't strictly for children. Many writers use journals and commit to writing in them daily. You may find this overwhelming, especially if you really want to spend your time writing a specific children's book.

Instead, consider writing in a journal to commemorate important events or family holidays. When my children began school, for example, I began writing about my experiences and emotions every time they started a new school year. Now I have a chronicle of that event. The writing has also helped me formulate my own perceptions of children's development and has led to numerous writing projects, both for children and for adults.

There are many other writing opportunities that you can take advantage of beyond journal writing. Consider writing articles for community newsletters or school publications. If you have a corporate newsletter at your office, consider submitting an article. Even writing a letter to the editor of your local paper means that you are stretching your writing muscles. Any writing you do will make you a better writer—even if it isn't writing that is directly related to writing for children.

Now let's consider the second part of the formula—submitting your work as often as possible. This is a little trickier. As we've seen in this book, submitting your work means taking a risk. But it also means you are increasing your publishing possibilities.

The best way to keep honest in the submission department is to create a schedule for submission. Pick an arbitrary day—the first Monday of every month, for example—and commit to submitting one manuscript, sending one query letter, or forwarding one proposal. You needn't always submit book-length work. Consider submitting to children's magazines, parenting magazines, or the other wide variety of publications discussed in this chapter.

If you commit to a regular submission schedule—and perhaps make a pact with a writing colleague that you will both stick to that schedule—you'll soon find that submitting your work feels natural. You'll let go of the fact that you are ultimately taking a risk. Submitting will feel businesslike and routine. (And before you know it, you will have mastered the art of effective cover and query letters. The more you write, the better you will get.)

This book has focused on the most popular forms of children's writing—fiction in picture books, early readers, chapter books, or middle grade or young adult novels. In order to fully take advantage of the formula, "write as much as you can, submit as often as you can," it's important to consider other categories of children's writing. There is a wide world of writing possibilities out there. By considering those opportunities and by developing new and creative ways to continue to explore the marketplace, you can stretch yourself as a writer and, quite possibly, achieve publishing success in an area that you never thought of.

GIVE YOURSELF CREDIT

Keep in mind that any writing credit you achieve will mean something to the editor who will review your next manuscript. A writing or publishing credit is a published piece of work—whether that work is a poem, a joke, a puzzle, or a nonfiction article. A publishing credit tells the editor who's reviewing your manuscript that you are able to write a piece that meets market specifications, revise and polish your writing so that it is worthy of being published, and you are actively submitting your work to publishers. It's an important credential, even if your credits aren't in the area that you ultimately want to publish in.

NONFICTION

Nonfiction is a genre that most writers don't think about when they approach writing for children. That may be because they remember the tedious informational books they had to read when they were younger. Today's nonfiction, however, is much more engaging than the musty, old encyclopedias you might have read as a child. And nonfiction can be just as creative to write.

The official definition of nonfiction is that it is factual or reference material. It requires solid research backed by a creative and engaging writing style that will pull the reader in. Good nonfiction inspires the reader to want to learn more about the topic after he has finished the book at hand.

Why Write Nonfiction?

Most bookstores and libraries are filled with fiction and nonfiction books. If you do a careful analysis of the offerings, you'll soon discover that there is substantially more nonfiction than fiction. In fact, it has been estimated that one-third of all books published are fiction while the remaining two-thirds are nonfiction. It has also been estimated that two-thirds of all writers want to write fiction, while one-third are amenable to nonfiction.

THE NONFICTION YARDSTICK

Good nonfiction meets the following standards:

Accuracy. The most important qualification of nonfiction is that it is accurate. The research needs to be solid. Nonfiction requires precise writing, even if that writing is on a general topic.

Inquiry. Good nonfiction inspires further inquiry on the part of the reader; after completing the book, he should be hungry for more information.

New perspective. If the subject is a familiar one, a nonfiction book should offer a fresh perspective on the topic.

Up-to-date. Nonfiction needs to be as up-to-date as possible. This is a particular challenge for writers who choose to write about scientific or technical topics.

Little or no anthropomorphism. Anthropomorphism can be quite subtle in a nonfiction book, but it should be avoided at all costs. Attributing human feelings to animals or inanimate objects is not appropriate in nonfiction.

Developmental appropriateness. The topic of interest should match the developmental needs of the reader. This is not only essential when it comes to the topic, but also when making comparisons in your narrative. A child younger than eight cannot comprehend size if it is only described in terms of inches, feet, and yards. Comparing size to something the child is familiar with, such as a school bus, will help them comprehend what that size really means.

Fact vs. fiction or theory. Good nonfiction makes a distinction between what is proven as factual and what is pure theory. Many good nonfiction books have fictional elements. A book about an earthquake, for example, may offer fictional diary entries from the perspective of a geologist, but it should be clear to the reader that these passages are distinct fiction passages. Just as important, theories should be presented as just that—theories—rather than a proven fact.

This suggests a simple truth: There is real opportunity in nonfiction. Perhaps nonfiction isn't what you've dreamed of writing, but it does offer a path to publication. Just as important, writing nonfiction will teach you about child development and story appeal. How do you make a topic fascinating to young readers? How do you draw them in? How do you structure the information so that it commands a reader's attention? How do you make young readers hunger for more information? These techniques are the same ones you will use to attract fiction readers. The difference is that you are pulling readers of nonfiction in with fact, while you are attracting readers of fiction with a compelling conflict that involves the characters in the story. Whether you are writing nonfiction or fiction, the challenge is the same.

Nonfiction is a rich and growing market, in part, because it is essential to today's educational standards. In order to pass the many required proficiency tests in schools, children must have the ability to read in content areas. That means they have to learn to comprehend passages in all kinds of subject areas—from science to history to math. Again, this offers the writer a unique opportunity.

Another advantage of writing nonfiction is that you can use the same research you complete for a nonfiction book to spark additional story ideas. Let's say you have decided to write a nonfiction book about the Alaskan dog race called the Iditarod. After you've written a proposal for the book and submitted it to a publisher, you can take what you know and outline a nonfiction article for a magazine. The subject may even inspire you to write a fictional picture book about that very dog race. With a single research project, you've actually developed three solid writing opportunities. And publishing success *is* publishing success. Whatever you publish can be added to your list of publishing credits and may open the door for your other titles.

Nonfiction is a genre category that offers very little risk. Most publishers prefer to receive proposals or queries for nonfiction instead of full manuscripts. You can prepare a proposal or a query letter in substantially less time than it takes to write a full manuscript. And if the publisher does not express interest on the basis of a query or a proposal, then you can choose an alternate publisher. If you happen to receive number of rejections, you can choose not to spend any additional time on the project.

Know the Elements

Most good nonfiction books contain elements that make it easier for children to find and comprehend the information included. The most basic of these are the index and glossary. Librarians, teachers, and, most importantly, editors expect to see these tools in a work of nonfiction. If your book is a longer work with chapters or if each page covers a different topic, you'll want to include a table of contents.

Other tools may also increase the appeal of your nonfiction work as well. These may include timelines, comprehension questions, special boxed features with more focused information, or sections of impressive facts and figures about the topic. They could also include a suggested reading list for further information.

While it may be tempting to include Web sites as one of your tools, exercise caution. URLs, the combination of words that connect readers to Web sites, change all the time. If you are not careful, you may direct your young readers to a Web

---

SOME UNIQUE ORGANIZATIONAL APPROACHES
_____

Chronological books progress through time from beginning to end.

True/false books explode popular myths about certain nonfiction topics. They might contain a single page that offers the myth—George Washington chopped down a cherry tree for example. On a facing page they may offer evidence that proves that the commonly accepted premise is false.

Now and then books rely on comparing the way things were done to the way things are done now.

Here and there books look at the same event as it is marked by two different cultures or two different societies. *Christmas in the Big House, Christmas in the Quarters* by Patricia C. McKissack and Fredrick L. McKissack, for instance, looks at parallel holiday celebrations in slave quarters and in the master's house.

Question and answer books start with simple questions, and use detailed narratives to answer the questions that are posed.

Alphabet books progress through a subject in alphabetic sequence. Consider developing an ABC book on baseball, soccer, or ballet. For older children, you can create a dictionary based on a particular subject: the dictionary of space, for example.

---

site that is inappropriate for children or even pornographic. Stick to Web sites from government organizations or established institutions that are likely to be around for a while. It is just as important is to show your readers how they might use the Web as a research tool, but make sure you guide them by suggesting key words and other research tools without actually referring to a specific Web site.

An attractive addition to a nonfiction book is an activity for further inquiry. Teachers and librarians call these add-on activities extensions. They allow the child to experience hands-on the topic you have explored in a book. If you are writing a book on percussion instruments, for example, you might include a section how to make percussion instruments. If you are proposing a series about children living in different countries, including a recipe for an ethnic food children can make will enhance the book's appeal to a publisher—and to a teacher, librarian, or parent.

Add Credibility

One way to add credibility to your nonfiction book is to make sure it follows educational guidelines. There are several national organizations that have created guidelines for the essential skills children need to know at certain age levels in certain curriculum areas. These include the National Teachers of Science, National Council of Teachers of Mathematics, The National Council of Teachers of English, the International Reading Association, and the National Association for the Education of Young Children. Your book doesn't have to meet every single one of the guidelines for every age level, but if you've covered some bases, you can enhance your chances of publication and your sales in the marketplace.

You can add credibility to your book by making other curriculum connections as well. If you are writing a book about a particular sport, for instance, make as many historical and science connections as possible. Can the swing of a baseball bat be compared to a basic physics concept, like a simple machine? What is the history of the sport you are exploring? What kind of multicultural connections can you make about that sport? (A form of the popular sport lacrosse, for example, was played by Native Americans as early as the 1600s. One of the greatest track and field stars of all time, Jesse Owens who broke numerous world records in the 1930s, was an African American.) The more connections you can make to school curriculum and social attitudes, the better chance your manuscript has.

Another way to add credibility is to consult experts in the field of the subject you are writing about. You may be an expert yourself, which will give you instant credibility. Make sure you mention these credentials in your query letter, proposal, and cover letter. Even if you are an expert, you'll want to consult other experts in your field to back up your opinion. And, if you aren't an expert, make sure you consult qualified experts—several of them—as you craft the details of your nonfiction piece.

Know the Categories

You're probably familiar with the standard categories of nonfiction, but there are some kinds of nonfiction books—or variations of nonfiction books—you may use everyday that you don't recognize as nonfiction. Here is a quick look at the basic types of nonfiction books:

Biography

One of the most popular forms of nonfiction is biography. Biographies reveal information about a contemporary or historical figure of great importance. They also give children insight into the kinds of lives other people lead; they provide important information about careers and accomplishments.

The important distinction between biography and other kinds of nonfiction is this: Children read biography as they do fiction. They look for a plot with a beginning, middle, and end. Because of that, the facts have to be organized the same way that they are in a fiction book—an introductory conflict, a series of episodes, and an ending that feels as if it is a resolution.

This will probably mean you will vary from a straight chronological retelling. In the biography I wrote about the actor Samuel L. Jackson, for instance, I started the book in the most critical point in Jackson's life—the moment he faced his own drug addiction. This was particularly appropriate because the book was directed at middle school readers. In my picture book biography of George Washington, I started at the moment George first met the older half brother who was such an important influence on his life and his career. Neither of these books started with the subject's birth. They started with a key episode that represented a conflict for the character and then worked backwards to fill in the details of their lives.

Like all nonfiction, biographies need to be impeccably researched. Invented dialogue, invented characters, or events that are not historically documented should not be included.

You can improve your chances of selling a biography by keeping track of important anniversaries. The anniversary of the Wright brothers' flight, for instance, offered a perfect opportunity to market a biography. If you plan to take advantage of an anniversary such as this, you need to start submitting your biography in advance of the event—at least three years, preferably four or five.

You can also enhance your biography's chances if you concentrate on why this particular individual is important to the age group you are writing for. The biography of Samuel L. Jackson I wrote was sold, in part, because, Jackson was scheduled to appear in a *Star Wars* movie. Up until that time, the movie for which he was most known was *Pulp Fiction*, hardly a movie that was appropriate for children.

If there is a timing issue that makes your topic particularly relevant, make sure you include this information in your cover letter, query letter, or proposal.

Fictionalized biographies differ from traditional biographies in that certain events are dramatized and certain aspects of the character's personality are invented. As long as the biography is identified as fictionalized, the author can invent passages of dialogue. The dialogue should have a basis in fact; it should be based on information found in journals, diaries, or other accounts.

A picture book biography can either be a straight biography or a fictionalized biography. Most often, they are fictionalized since they need to contain visual action that may not be entirely historically accurate.

The Photo Essay

A photo essay is a nonfiction work in which the information is imparted through photographs as well as through text. If you are a reasonable photographer, you can supply photographs as part of your manuscript submission or you can offer to supply photographs in a query or a proposal. You can also offer to acquire photographs for the publisher and take on the financial responsibility of photo research. This will give you an advantage. Most publishers have photo research staffs, but they are often overworked. Offering to do the work yourself can enhance your position.

When you acquire photographs, you can rely on photo agencies; there are also a great many free sources of photographs. If you are producing a book on any commercial activity, for instance, it's likely you can contact major companies for publicity photos. There are also many government agencies—like NASA—that will provide photos at little or no cost. (These photos aren't technically free; they are paid for through our tax dollars, after all!)

Activity Books

Activity books take the form of cookbooks, science experiment books, craft books, and any other how-to titles. These books are popular in libraries, schools, bookstores, and specialty markets. Craft books—especially those that tie into a holiday, educational concepts, or items that are readily available—are especially popular. The increasing number of craft store outlets has only added to the viability of these books.

Science Topics

Science topics are popular topics for nonfiction books, especially science books for a younger age group. Teachers of students in younger grades rely on books about science topics to enhance children's knowledge and natural inquiry. Children in lower grades also latch on to science topics as they are presented in nonfiction picture book form. How many young readers do you know, for instance, who read everything they can about certain subjects—whether that subject is cars and trucks, dinosaurs, or ballet?

Social Studies and History Topics

Social studies and history topics are also popular themes. When exploring these topics, it's important once again to keep in mind the various stages of child development. Children learn social studies concepts this way: They understand their immediate surroundings (their home), and then move onto their street, community, town, and state. First graders may know what their state capital is, but they don't fully comprehend distance, culture, and history unless it is made directly relevant to their own lives. That's why history and social studies aren't introduced as official school subjects until third grade.

Reference and Trivia

There are many books that focus on facts and details, both the minute details that fascinate kids and the more general details. Almanacs and "everything" books are good examples of these. *The World Almanac For Kids*, produced by Facts on File, is one of the best-selling nonfiction books for kids. That's because it is not only a reference guide but also a browsable guide chock-full of "gee whiz" facts. Book that include all kinds of facts about an individual topic are bound to be popular, but the topic of consideration should be one kids are interested in and participate in.

The Nonfiction Query/Proposal

Before you sit down to write your actual query letter or proposal, you need to answer some important questions about your topic and your overall goals. Why is this topic important to the targeted audience? The reasons can vary—the topic could be part of their school curriculum or it could just be a subject that kids are interested in. The best nonfiction topics offer a combination of both. The subject of dinosaurs, for example, is both incredibly popular with young readers and is also a part of the school curriculum.

How will you deal with the topic in a new or different way? If your topic is one that has extensive coverage in the marketplace, you will need to detail for the publisher how your approach is unique or different from what is already available.

What tools will you include? You already know to include a glossary and an index. What else will you include to make your subject more accessible?

What are your credentials and what experts have you consulted? This is an

NONFICTION: A CASE STUDY

My book *The Exxon Valdez* published by Chelsea House in 2000 was part of the World Disaster series aimed at readers from sixth to ninth grade. Most of these readers were babies and toddlers—or not even born—when the Valdez hit an underground reef and spilled millions of gallons of oil into the ocean off the southern coast of Alaska on the Valdez peninsula. In 2000, there were much more serious threats than an oil crisis, after all, especially in the minds of middle and high school readers. And the whole notion of a nonrenewable resource would be a difficult on to explain to readers who perceived themselves as immortal.

The first thing I did was identify my audience—young people who were interested in the environment. It also included teachers, like science and history teachers, who were asking students to write reports on the topic. And it included librarians who wanted to make sure that school library collection was well balanced.

I had to decide what themes I should develop that would connect with both middle and high school kids. First, I had to list the facts:

The captain of the ship was impaired by alcohol.

The oil was leaving Alaska via the Alaskan pipeline, which had environmental implications.

The sleepy town of Valdez, bolstered by the oil industry blossomed economically due to the disaster.

Native Americans, who hunt and eat fish and animals, were the most affected.

The whole thing would not have happened had there not been such a need for oil.

Suddenly, I had some themes to work with that made sense.

Alcohol abuse and personal responsibility. This is a theme young adults hear over and over again; what could I do in this book to really make it hit home?

Preservation of the environment and technological advances. Here, I could appeal to a young person's own experiences with nature. What would happen if a factory invaded their favorite park? How would they feel if a power plant was built next to the summer camp they attended as a child?

Communities and economic growth. Most small towns—and even medium-sized cities—can be affected by isolated economic factors. In the case of Valdez, the town had grown first because of the pipeline. Its economic growth after the disaster, however, was even more dramatic. The rescue and clean-up workers who arrived after the wreck spent money and contributed to the economy. After they left, the town was in better shape than it had been before the disaster. It is now a major tourist attraction. Here was something I could offer that was a new idea: The great tragedy of the Valdez disaster actually contributed to the growth and health of the community.

Native American culture and the destruction of nature. The tragic sight of an otter covered with oil might draw in many young people. Native Americans rely on hunting and fishing to feed themselves and their families. Even when the Exxon company offered them free food, they did not accept it. Hunting and fishing was more than a means of subsistence. It represented pride. Young adults have their own sense of pride. I knew if I could make this connection effectively, the book would work.

The need for oil and the United States consumption of this resource. This was the hardest concept to put into terms that young adults could understand. Most towns and small cities do not have effective public transportation systems. The car is still the main transportation vehicle, and getting a driver's license is a rite of passage for most young people. It means a newfound independence. It also means we are ultimately going to have to depend on foreign sources of oil—a situation fraught with political implications.

Continued next page

> **Why was all of this analysis so important?** Ultimately, because it defined the kind of book I was to write. I wasn't writing a book about the Exxon Valdez. The disaster was a backdrop for exploring the themes of the event—themes young adults could relate to. Every chapter dealt with some aspect of personal responsibility, the environment, economic issues, cultural traditions, and the implications of relying on foreign oil. The book became stronger because of its emphasis on the issues rather than on the event itself.

important issue with nonfiction, and you should be confident in your source material. This will indicate that you have confidence in the accuracy of your research.

OTHER OPPORTUNITIES

There are other significant opportunities for children's writers who are willing to stretch themselves beyond traditional boundaries. To get a sense of what is available, all you have to do is consider the various forms of the written word that are aimed at children.

While they have declined significantly in recent years, children's magazines continue to offer opportunities for children's writers. Many of these magazines, like *Cricket* and *Highlights for Children*, for instance, are general interest. Others, like *Ranger Rick* (science) and *Calliope* (history), are more specialized. Most children's magazines publish nonfiction articles and many publish fiction as well. Children's magazines have the most difficulty finding what are called "fillers"—puzzles, games, jokes, profiles, and trivia information they use between their major stories.

To get a sense of children's magazines and their needs, first visit your local library's children's magazine section. Sample their wares and determine whether the magazine's profile is special interest or general interest. Copy down the titles for the articles that each magazine features. Then, use your *Children's Writer's & Illustrator's Market* to explore each magazine further. Finally, of course, request writer's guidelines, either by visiting the Web site or by writing a letter. Many children's magazines also publish editorial calendars that feature the subject matter they intend to offer each week. (Note that many children's magazines offer their magazines online rather than ink-on-paper. Some magazines offer both online and print versions.)

Parent magazines also offer opportunities for writers of children's work. Parent magazines often include a children's section, with articles aimed at children. Your local community probably has a parent's magazine. Pick one up and discover what kinds of articles it has to offer.

There are other opportunities to market your work. Educational publishers are in the market for writers to produce both nonfiction and fiction materials. There are specialized publishers for the inspirational market. Their needs range from summer Bible School curriculum to picture books.

The best way to discover opportunities is to become sensitive to them. Every day—in every place you visit—there are written materials aimed at children. Investigate them and discover a new, untapped opportunity.

MORE SIMPLE INSPIRATION

There is one more ingredient in the formula for becoming a children's writer: Write as much as you can, submit as often as you can, and *give back as much as you can*. One important way you can learn about writing is to give to your community through writing. How can you do that? Consider these options.

Literacy Programs

Volunteering in literacy programs will help you learn how children acquire reading skills and will also ensure that there is always an audience for children's literature and literature in general. It's a simple fact that if children can't achieve a fundamental level of literacy they won't succeed. They also won't likely become enthusiasts (and consumers) of literature as children or as adults. Furthering the cause of literacy is furthering the cause of education and literature.

There are many opportunities to volunteer for literacy organizations. You can teach English as a second language even if you do not have command of a second language. You can volunteer at schools, helping young children to read. Family literacy programs that instruct entire families in reading are gaining widespread attention. These programs are held at churches, libraries, and schools, and are always in need of volunteers.

In addition to literacy programs that offer hands-on opportunities, there are organizations that work to put books into the hands of children who need them. Organizations like First Book also help young parents understand how valuable reading is to the brain development of their child.

Young Adult Programs

Young adults frequently turn to writing to express their frustrations about growing up, their interpersonal needs, and their opinions and feelings. Writing, quite simply, gives them a voice to express what they are feeling.

Fostering this voice is a powerful thing. It's likely there are writing programs in your community geared to teenagers. It's also probable that many of these programs offer little more than the opportunity to express teenage angst. Volunteering in these programs as an expert can help bring the tools of writing—plot, character, and setting—to the table. Teaching young adults that good writing is more than their feelings written down on paper is a valuable experience. It can help you and the writers you work with come to a new understanding of how to turn emotion into craft.

Senior Citizen Programs

Seniors are full of stories that they want to record. These stories may take the form of memories from their childhood or they may be family stories that have been passed down for generations. There are many opportunities to volunteer to help seniors commit these stories to paper—and to posterity. And, in so doing, you may be inspired by the subject matter or the era. You may also be inspired to seek out experiences in your own life or family that may provide fodder for a new story or book.

The Library

If you are like most people who like books and writing, you probably spend a lot of time at your local library. Volunteering at your library—especially at the local school library—is a great way to learn about the latest books.

Volunteering at a library can take a number of forms. You might shelve books, which allows you to see the most recent books for children. You can also participate by helping with library story times. At story hour, you can see firsthand how children react to books.

Special Facilities

There are likely programs in your community that support writers in other nontraditional settings—prisons, local community shelters, YMCAs/YWCAs, etc. These programs are generally closely controlled and entirely safe, especially if they are administered by an agency or other organization. When you volunteer to facilitate writing in these places, you are doing more than just teaching a writing class. You are offering a voice to those who don't have voices. These experiences can be difficult—they are among the most difficult I have attempted—but I always emerge with story ideas I wouldn't have had if I had simply sat at my computer. And I always came back with a renewed sense of what writing really means—whether for children or adults.

Literary Centers

Many communities have literary centers that offer public readings, writing classes, experiences with authors, and the like. Becoming involved at a literary center, either as a hands-on volunteer or in a fund-raising capacity, will probably allow you to meet professional writers, as well as writers who are your peers. Many of these centers are in smaller communities and some are focused on children's writers.

THE GRANDEST DREAM

The goal of this book has been to offer inspirational advice and practical tips. My grandest hope, however, is that you have come to see yourself as a writer of children's books. There are many, many events and issues that influence our lives, but children's writers look at life through a special lens, always searching for new story ideas while at the same time nurturing the children who are their audience through the power of words.

Keep children at the center of your writing life. Know that they need good literature. They need to master reading, and they need to see themselves and their conflicts on the pages of your books. When you get rejection letters, remind yourself of the important work that you are doing and stick to it. Our children deserve the best we can give them. Hone your craft so that you can give them your gifts.

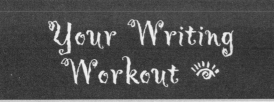

FEELINGS, FEELINGS!

Rewrite the phrases below that reflect opinion—feelings rather than fact. I have completed the first one for you.

Hummingbirds love brightly colored flowers.

Bird experts report that hummingbirds are attracted by brightly colored flowers.

A bear's favorite foods are fish and honey.

George Washington was frightened by the wide expanse of the river.

Tourists love the art museums in Paris.

The weather in Alaska is horrible.

LOOK IT UP!

Examine the Web sites for:

National Council of Teachers of Mathematics (www.nctm.org)
National Council of Teachers of English (www.ncte.org)
International Reading Association (www.reading.org)
National Science Teachers Association (www.nsta.org)

NARROW IT DOWN

Come up with three nonfiction book ideas. Think of five activities that kids are interested in. I've suggested one for you.

Baseball

Now take the topics and brainstorm five ideas in a different nonfiction category.

Activity: How to collect and display baseball cards

Biography: Sammy Sousa

Photo essay: A Day in the life of a batboy

Science: How a baseball bat is made

Social Studies: How baseball is played in Japan

THE TOP TEN

Research the "top ten" in a category that kids are interested in. Consider the top ten soccer players or the top ten most devastating world disasters. Think about ways that you can create an "almanac" stylebook based on what you have developed.

GETTING TO KNOW YOU: BIOGRAPHY EXERCISE

Write down ten people you want to know more about. Make as many connections as you can between the people you have selected and children. Here is an example:

Martha Washington

She probably moved to North America as a child, why?

What was her young life in America like?

WRITE WHAT YOU KNOW

While writing what you know may not be the best advice for writing fiction, it is the key to writing nonfiction. Make a list of things you know about and determine how these topics might become a children's book. Here are some examples:

Swimming

Water polo

History of water polo

WRITING GROUP GRABBER

Pick a single nonfiction topic. Assign each member of the group a different approach. Consider alphabet book, trivia, photo essay, question and answer, now and then, true and false, here and there. Share the results of your writing.

GLOSSARY

Acquisition ı In business, this term describes what happens when one company buys out another company. Acquisition in publishing also refers to the act of acquiring a manuscript from an author to publish.

Activity Book ı A book that offers activities children can do. These may take the form of books of puzzles or craft activities or science experiments.

Advance ı An amount of money paid to a writer or illustrator that is charged against their royalties. Advances are often paid in installments.

Anthropomorphism ı Stories that attribute human characteristics to animals.

Backlist ı A publisher's offering of titles that have been promoted during previous years but are still in print.

Book Development House ı A company that develops manuscripts and illustrators for specific book projects to "sell" to publishers.

Book Proposal ı A book proposal generally consists of a synopsis, outline, and the first three sample chapters.

Booksellers ı The publishing industry's term for bookstores.

Bookstore Chain ı A large chain of bookstores, such as Barnes & Noble or Borders.

Chapter Book ı A book for readers in the early primary grades that contains simple language and self-contained chapters.

Character Growth ı The way a character grows and changes as a result of confronting the events in the plot.

Concept Book ı A book for preschoolers and early school children that teaches or reinforces an educational concept or addresses a childhood problem.

Conflict ı The story's central problem, introduced in the opening lines. The main character confronts this problem as the plot unfolds.

Copyright ı The right of an author or an illustrator to protect their work from being copied.

Cover Letter ı A letter that accompanies a manuscript submission that introduces the story and the author to the publisher.

Demographics ı The study of population trends. Demographics can indicate how many readers there are for picture books, chapter books, middle grade readers, and young adult novels at any one point in time.

Dialogue ı The verbal interplay between characters in a story.

Early Reader ı An early reader uses a variety of techniques: controlled vocabulary, predictable passages, and cumulative stories to help young readers grasp early literacy concepts.

Emergent Reader ı A young child, usually in kindergarten or first grade, who is beginning to read.

Empathy ı The feeling of identification that the reader has for the main character in a story.

End Caps ı Displays that are attached to the ends of bookshelves.

English as a Second Language | Programs that are designed to teach English to those who are not fluent in the language.

Face Out | The term used to describe books that are positioned with their covers facing outward.

Family Literacy Programs | Programs that engage families, often families for whom English is not their native language, to read and speak fluently.

Federal Funding | Funding that flows from the federal government to support various programs. Federal funding supports purchases of books by libraries, school libraries, and schools.

Fictionalized Biography | A biography that contains some elements that are not verified through primary or secondary sources. Dialogue, for example, is often invented in fictionalized biographies.

First-Person Narrative | Telling a story through the eyes of the main character by using the pronoun "I" for that main character. First-person narrative provides a personal account of the events of the plot.

Fluent Reader | An older child, generally in second through fourth grade, who is reading without assistance.

Folktale | A story originally passed verbally through generations of a single culture.

Foot Traffic | The number of customers who enter retail outlets. Increased foot traffic means increased sales.

Frontlist | The books a publisher promotes during their current season. They generally receive a publisher's strongest financial endorsement.

General Adjectives | Adjectives—such as beautiful, nice, and handsome—that have unspecific meanings.

Genre | A category of literature, such as mystery, fantasy, or poetry.

Juvenile Publishing | Another term for children's publishing.

Illustrator | An artist who has been trained to illustrate a narrative. An illustrator knows the media to work in and how to hone in on the right visual detail, has a keen eye for perspective, and is able to replicate the same character over and over.

Imprint | A line of books from a particular publisher. The books generally have a distinct theme or voice.

Inspirational | A category of books that inspires a renewal or a new understanding of faith, usually founded in Christian ideals or culture.

Institutional Books | Books that are sold primarily to libraries, school libraries, or other institutions. These books are usually hardcover with special reinforced binding.

Internal Dialogue | A character's thoughts written in the style of speech.

"It Was All A Dream" Ending | An ending in which the main character discovers that the events of the plot didn't really happen. Often, this kind of ending is left slightly ambiguous; there may be an object left from the

dream sequence that hints that the "dream" might have really happened. These endings cheat the reader out of a true resolution.

Literacy Programs | Programs that depend on trained professionals and volunteers to teach reading skills to those who need them.

Main Character | The character in a story who faces the main conflict and grows and changes as a result of the confict's resolution.

Market Guides | Guides written especially for writers that indicate what kind of books publishers are interested in.

Mass-Market Books | Books that are produced for a large audience, generally in paperback form, and sold in markets other than bookstores.

Merger | When two companies combine their interests to become one.

Middle Grade Novels | Novels for readers in grades three through six.

Minor Characters | Characters who are part of the plot, but do nothing to control the plot's action.

Multicultural Literature | Fiction about a racial or ethnic group that is culturally or socially different from most middle-class values found in literature for children.

Multiple Submission | A manuscript an author sends to several publishers at one time. Also called a simultaneous submission.

North American Rights | Rights to publish and sell books created by foreign publishers in North America. Most American publishers buy foreign rights to various properties. American publishers are also in the business of selling these rights to publishers overseas.

Novelty Book | A book that relies on a novelty of some sort. Pop-ups and lift-a-flaps are examples of novelty books.

Omniscient Narrator | The "invisible" storyteller who tells the story, but is not invested in the story itself.

Over the Transom | A term used to describe manuscripts that arrive at a publisher without earlier solicitation. An unsolicited manuscript.

Personification | Turning an inanimate object into a human-like object in a fictional work.

Photo Essay | A work of nonfiction that consists of narrative explanation and photographs that provide information about a topic or a process.

Plot | The events of a story. Stories for children typically have three episodes or major events, each building in intensity.

Prewriting | Planning the basic building blocks of your story by developing preliminary ideas about the plot, characters, and setting.

Promotion | The public relations and advertising campaign a publisher uses to promote sales of a title.

Publisher's Guidelines | Individual guides provided by publishers, updated frequently, to indicate what kinds of books they are interested in and how they would like to receive them.

Publisher's Sales Representative | An individual who is employed by a publisher to sell books to bookstores and distributors.

Query Letter | A letter that is sent in advance of a manuscript that solicits interest from a publisher in that manuscript.

Readability | The reading level of a book or story.

Resolution | The solution to the plot's problem. The solution should inspire character growth.

Royalty | A percentage of the proceeds of book sales paid to the author by the publisher.

Secondary Characters | Characters who are directly involved in the action of the plot but aren't the direct focus of the story.

Show, Don't Tell | A writing technique in which a writer shows a situation or character through actions rather than through detailed description.

Simultaneous Submission | See *Multiple Submission*.

Slush Pile | The slang name for the "pile" of unsolicited manuscripts.

Story Book | A picture book that tells a story chronologically, with a beginning, a body, and an end.

Synopsis | A summary of a work usually included in a proposal.

Theme | The overriding idea of a story or a book.

Third Person Narrative | Telling a story without using "I" as the narrator, using a narrator who seems to be uninvolved in the story, but actually is telling the story the way he wants it told.

Titles | The publishing industry's term for books.

Trade Books | Books sold primarily to bookstores and libraries.

Trade Magazines | Magazines that serve a particular industry. In the children's publishing industry, *Publisher's Weekly* and *School Library Journal* are the major trade publications.

Turn-Around Tale | A story that relies on characters or plot that are the opposite of what they would normally appear.

Unsolicited Manuscript | A manuscript sent by an author to a publisher without prior solicitation by the publisher.

Viewpoint | The action and emotion of a story as seen by a single character. The main character should be the viewpoint character.

Vocabulary | A selection of words appropriate for a particular age reader.

Workable First Draft | A draft that has enough of a developed story line that it can be revised.

Writer's Guidelines | (also called Publisher's Guidelines). Guidelines publishers provide to writers to indicate what kinds of manuscripts they are looking for and how they like to see manuscripts presented.

Writing Credit | A published piece of writing.

Young Adult Novel | A novel aimed at readers from the ages of ten and up. These books deal with the critical passage from teen to adult.

RESOURCES AND RECOMMENDED READING

Books About Writing and Publishing Children's Books

Children's Writer's & Illustrator's Market, Alice Pope, editor

Creating Characters Kids Will Love, Elaine Marie Alphin

It's a Bunny-Eat-Bunny World, Olga Litowinsky

Picture Writing, Anastasia Suen

Story Sparkers, Debbie Dadey and Marcia Thornton Jones

Ten Steps to Publishing Children's Books, Berthe Amoss and Eric Suben

The Way to Write for Children, Joan Aiken

Worlds of Children, William Zinsser

Writer's Guide to Crafting Stories for Children, Nancy Lamb

Writing Books for Children, Jane Yolen

Writing Books for Young People, James Cross Giblin

Writing for Children and Teenagers, Lee Wyndham and Arnold Madison

Writing with Pictures, Uri Shulevitz

Writing Young Adult Novels, Hadley Irwin and Jeannette Eyerly

Books About Children's Books and Children's Literature

An Introduction to Children's Literature: Children's Books of the 19th century, Lou W. McCulloch

Battling Dragons: Issues and Controversy in Children's Literature, Susan Lehr

Dear Genius: The Selected Letters of Ursula Nordstrom, Leonard S. Marcus, editor

Don't Tell the Grown-Ups, Alison Lurie

The Essential Guide to Children's Books and Their Creators, Anita Silvey, editor

Exploding the Myths: The Truth About Teenagers and Reading, Marc Aronson

From Dr. Mather to Dr. Seuss: Two Hundred Years of American Books for Children

Picture Books for Children, Patricia Cicanciolo

Through the Eyes of A Child: An Introduction to Children's Literature, Donna E. Norton and Sandra E. Norton

Written for Children: An Outline of Children's Literature, John Rowe Townsend

Books About Technique

The Chicago Manual of Style, The University of Chicago Press

Children's Writer's Word Book, Alijandra Mogliner

The Elements of Style, William Strunk and E.B. White

The Writer's Essential Desk Reference, 2d edition, the editors of Writer's Digest Books

Writing Dialogue, Tom Chiarella

Books About Writing and Creativity

Bird by Bird: Some Instructions on Writing and Life, Anne Lamott

The Courage to Write, How Writer's Transcend Fear, Ralph Keyes

Drawing on the Right Side of the Brain: A Course in Enhancing Creativity and Artistic Confidence, Betty Edwards

How to Write With the Skill of a Master and the Genius of a Child, Marshall J. Cook

On Writing, Stephen King

Walking on Alligators: A Book of Meditations for Writers, Susan Shaughnessy

What If? Writing Exercises for Fiction Writers, Anne Bernays and Pamela Painter

Writing Down the Bones: Freeing the Writer Within, Natalie Goldberg

Newsletters and Periodicals

Booklist (www.ala.org/booklist/)
  American Library Association
  50 E. Huron Street
  Chicago, IL 60611
Children's Book Insider (www.write4kids.com)
  Write4Kids.com
  901 Columbia Road
  Fort Collins, CO 80440
Children's Writer (www.childrenswriter.com)
  The Institute of Children's Literature
  93 Long Ridge Road
  West Redding, CT 06896-0811
The Horn Book (www.hbook.com)
  56 Roland Street
  Suite 200
  Boston, MA 02129
Publishers Weekly (www.publishersweekly.com)
  360 Park Avenue South
  New York, NY 10010
School Library Journal (www.slj.com)
  American Library Association
  50 E. Huron Street
  Chicago, IL 60611
SCBWI Bulletin (www.scbwi.org)
  Society for Children's Book Writers and Illustrators
  8271 Beverly Boulevard
  Los Angeles, CA 90048

Book Guides and Directories

Award-Winning Books for Children and Adults, Betty L. Criscoe and Philip J. Lanasa

Children's Books in Print, R.R. Bowker

Choosing Books for Children, Betsy Hearne

Magazines for Children: A Guide for Parents, Teachers, and Librarians, American
   Library Association

Subject Guide to Children's Books in Print, R.R. Bowker

Organizations

American Booksellers Association (www.ambook.org)
   828 South Broadway
   Tarrytown, NY 10591

American Library Association (www.ala.org)
   50 E. Huron Street
   Chicago, IL 60611

The Association of Authors Representatives (www.aar-online.org)
   P.O. Box 237201
   Ansonia Station, New York, NY 10003

Children's Book Council (www.cbcbooks.org)
   12 West Thirty-seventh Street
   Second Floor
   New York, NY 10018

Children's Literature Association (http://ebbs.english.vt.edu/chla/)
   P.O. Box 138
   Battle Creek, MI 49016-0138

The Institute of Children's Literature (www.institutechildrenslit.com)
   93 Long Ridge Road
   West Redding, CT 06896

International Reading Association (www.reading.org)
   800 Barksdale Rd, P.O. Box 81396021
   Newark, DE 19714

The Society of Children's Book Writers and Illustrators (www.scbwi.org)
   8271 Beverly Boulevard
   Los Angeles, CA 90048

INDEX